THE
WHITE BARN INN
COOKBOOK

FOUR SEASONS AT
THE CELEBRATED AMERICAN INN

Recipes by Jonathan Cartwright

Text by Susan Sully

Photographs by Philippe Schaff

RUNNING PRESS
PHILADELPHIA · LONDON

ACKNOWLEDGMENTS

This book could not have been created without the enthusiasm, hard work, and generosity of many individuals and local Maine businesses. Much gratitude is owed to Dannah Fine Flowers in Kennebunkport for floral displays, Villeroy & Boch in Kittery for fine tableware, J. Jorgensen Antiques in Wells for fine antiques, Rocky Mountain Antique Quilts in York for quilts, and Victorian Affair in Kennebunkport for a peignoir— thank you for contributing to the exquisite settings for this book. Thanks to Snug Harbor Farm in Kennebunk and Patton's Berry Stand in Kennebunkport for seasonal color and produce, and to the Maritime Museum of Kennebunkport for the use of its dock. Thanks are also due to the Kennebunkport American Legion for presenting the Memorial Day parade, to the Franciscan Monastery for hosting the Christmas Carol program of the Christmas Prelude, and to the Kennebunk, Kennebunkport Chamber of Commerce for organizing the Christmas Prelude and the Blessing of the Fleet, events featured in the pages of this book that enrich the life of our community. Special thanks are offered to the staff of the Brick Store Museum in Kennebunk for sharing their treasure trove of historical information about the history of the region. And finally, deep gratitude is due to the staff of the White Barn Inn, as well as its sister properties Grissini, Stripers, Schooners, the Beach House, the Yachtsman Lodge and Marina, and the Breakwater Inn, for all the hard work and dedication to craft.

© 2003 by Glenrohan, Inc.
All rights reserved under the Pan-American and
    International Copyright Conventions
Printed in China

This book may not be reproduced in whole or in part, in any form or by any means, electronic or mechanical, including photocopying, recording, or by any information storage and retrieval system now known or hereafter invented, without written permission from the publisher.

9 8 7 6 5 4 3 2 1
Digit on the right indicates the number of this printing

Library of Congress Control Number: 2002095690
ISBN 0-7624-1595-9

Cover and interior design by Frances J. Soo Ping Chow
Edited by Janet Bukovinsky Teacher
Typography: Bickham Script, ITC Berkeley,
    and Schneidlers Initials

This book may be ordered by mail from the publisher.
Please include $2.50 for postage and handling.
But try your bookstore first!

Running Press Book Publishers
125 South Twenty-second Street
Philadelphia, Pennsylvania 19103-4399

Visit us on the web!
www.runningpress.com

TABLE OF CONTENTS

Introduction 5

Spring 17

A Spring Celebration at the White Barn Inn 23

A Springtime Picnic 48

A Spring Cocktail 56

A Spring Seafood Menu 57

Breakfast by the Pool 73

Summer 83

Fourth of July Party 89

A Simple Boating Lunch 106

A Summer Tea Party 113

A Summer Seafood Dinner 122

A Summer Cocktail 138

Autumn 141

Thanksgiving Day Dinner 147

Day after Thanksgiving Driving Tour Picnic 167

A Fall Vegetarian Dinner 172

A Romantic Fireside Dinner 190

Winter 201

Winter by the Sea 207

Christmas Prelude Dinner at the White Barn Inn 217

A Holiday Cocktail Party 236

A New Year's Day Brunch 249

Source Guide 259

Index 260

Welcome to
THE WHITE BARN INN

⁂

"This cozy little place is becoming very popular with its guests who enjoy home comforts, large cool rooms and an excellent table. [The proprietor] knows how to run a house of this kind to perfection." Although this description of the White Barn Inn was written in 1887, when Kennebunkport, Maine, was just gaining popularity as a fashionable seaside resort, it still perfectly expresses the appeal of this establishment that marries luxury with simplicity and tradition with contemporary flair. Established in 1887 as the Forest Hill House, the inn quickly attracted an upscale clientele that sought refuge from the summer heat and hectic lifestyle of nearby Boston and Portsmouth. Today the White Barn Inn, built during the heyday of America's resort movement, is one of only forty exclusive Relais & Château hotels in America. With a Relais Gourmand restaurant that is one of just three in New England to win the AAA Five Diamond award, the White Barn Inn is still recognized as the one of the region's finest lodgings and restaurants.

A nineteenth-century country house with an adjacent barn that gives the property its name, the inn combines rustic Maine ambience with European-style service and innovative New England cuisine. Fresh flowers add vibrant color in spring and summer. Fires burn in the living room hearths of the main house throughout fall and winter. Windows frame constantly changing views of each season's particular beauties, while the seasonal bounty is celebrated in gourmet presentations every night at the restaurant. With this book the staff of the White Barn Inn share the secrets of their special brand of hospitality with readers who wish to recall the delights of a holiday in Maine, re-create the pleasures they experienced at the White Barn Inn at home, or simply travel in their imaginations to one of the most sought-after resorts in America.

A Brief History
of Kennebunkport and the
White Barn Inn

Long before Europeans landed on the shores of Kennebunk Beach, Native Americans populated the region, hunting game on the Kennebunk Plains and harvesting the fruits of forest and sea. French and English explorers first visited the area's rocky shoreline and sandy beaches in the early 1600s, establishing fishing camps and trading posts by the 1620s. Early settlers began cutting local white pine and hardwoods, and by 1640 they established a shipbuilding and shipping trade that flourished for 250 years. Ships sailed from the mouth of the Kennebunk River to Boston, New York, and Philadelphia and across the seas to the West Indies,

Europe, and the Far East. More than 300 wooden sailing vessels were built in Kennebunk and Kennebunkport between 1854 and 1918, when the last of the great ships, a four-masted schooner called the Kennebunk, was launched into the sea.

Although the region's importance as a shipbuilding center had begun to dwindle by the end of the nineteenth century, a powerful new "industry" started to gain force by the mid-1800s: resort development. During the nineteenth century northeastern America became the home of thriving cities where industrialization changed the pace of life, ushering in a host of "modern" conveniences while creating a noisy, urban environment. Upper-middle-class city dwellers began to dream of escaping to the country or the shore, where they could reconnect with nature. The development of rail travel made it possible for them to travel with ease to formerly remote locations.

In 1872 a branch line of the Boston & Maine Railroad offered stops along a route from South Berwick to Portland, including a new station in Kennebunk. Suddenly, Bostonians discovered that they could reach the unspoiled beaches and charming old town of Kennebunk in a three-hour train ride. A group of Boston and Kennebunkport businessmen recognized the potential of this transportation development and quickly purchased several hundred acres of land along the coast that spread out on either side of the Kennebunk River. Doing business as the Boston and Kennebunkport Seashore Company, these developers built the grand Ocean Bluff Hotel on a hill (now the site of the Colony

Hotel) and offered for sale lots of lands subdivided for hotels and seasonal cottages.

Many more guesthouses and inns were established during the early decades of the resort movement, including the Forest Hill House, which would be renamed the White Barn Inn in the late twentieth century. Constructed in 1820 in a typical New England style, the building was purchased in the mid-1880s by the Boothby family, who transformed it into an inn, operating from spring through early fall, catering mainly to a Jewish clientele. The Boothbys divided the upper floors into large, well-appointed guestrooms and added a wraparound porch with Victorian details. On the ground floor they created spacious living and dining rooms cooled by summer breezes and warmed by wood-burning fires in autumn and spring. By 1887 the establishment was already celebrated through word of mouth and in the press as an extraordinary inn providing excellent accommodations and dining.

UNCOMMON CHARM

Today the common rooms of the White Barn Inn retain their old-fashioned appeal, with nineteenth-century-

been left unfinished, their timbers aged to a rich dark brown. Two walls have been replaced with picture windows that frame views of a walled garden and the surrounding landscape, which changes color and mood with each season. Starched white linen tablecloths, polished silver place settings, and glistening crystal stemware provide refined counterpoint to the interior. Above the tables former haylofts are filled with country antiques that glow beneath soft lights.

During the early years of the resort movement, the Seashore Company promoted the area including Kennebunk Beach, Kennebunkport, and Cape Arundel as an exclusive destination, inviting "none but the elite of cottagers to locate here." Their advertisements described the area as one "possessing natural scenery, such,

inspired upholstery and wallpapers, antique portraits, and oriental carpets laid across hardwood floors. The guestrooms combine traditional furnishings and decorations with such up-to-date luxuries as spa bathroom fixtures and gas-burning fires. An annex of spacious rooms and cottagelike suites, though constructed only recently, captures the same charm that characterizes the original inn and blends easily into the woods that surround the hilltop property. The inn's newest room, the Loft, nestles in the gables of the white barn that gives the property its name and features contemporary design and a large spa bathroom.

The main floor of the barn has been transformed into a dining room that marries rustic architecture with elegant accoutrements. Interior walls and trusses have

as perhaps, no other similar portion on the New England coast possesses." They extolled its "rugged beauty of scenery, delightful boating and bathing, abundant fishing, and convenient hotel accommodations. . . ." Within fifteen years a dozen large hotels were constructed in prime locations along the waterfront, and seasonal homes called "cottages"—a term that referred more to their fanciful architecture than to their scale—were built.

In addition to its natural charms, the area boasted Colonial- and Federal-style houses built by affluent chandlers and merchants of the eighteenth and early nineteenth centuries. By the late nineteenth century, Americans already disillusioned by the Industrial Age were intrigued by these antiquated buildings. Artists flocked to Kennebunkport to capture the charms of the old structures on canvas and paper, while architects, interior designers, and landscape designers of the Colonial Revival movement invoked the old-fashioned simplicity of these wooden houses in new cottages built for a wealthy clientele. By freely mixing elements inspired by Colonial architecture with the emerging Queen Anne style, they created the rambling Shingle Style houses for which Maine's coastline is now famous.

VARIOUS SOURCES OF AMUSEMENT

Just as Kennebunkport's architecture blended the old with the new, satisfying the desire for both nostalgia and fashion, so did its entertainments and pastimes. A typical advertisement from the Wentworth House hotel describes "[a] new 30-foot Yacht ready to take parties to sail or fish. Excellent facilities for Sailing, Bathing, Fishing and Driving, with Bowling Alleys and various sources of amusement. Horses and Carriages to let; also

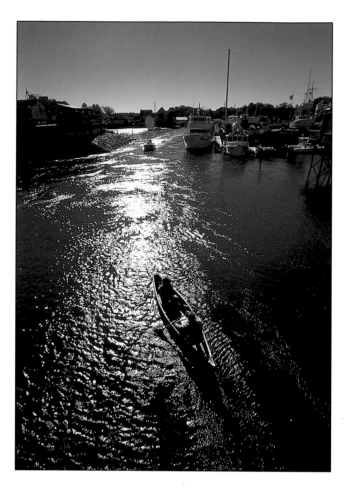

with recommendations for outings to consider. Suggestions might include sea-bound whale-watching excursions, hiking and biking tours, deep-sea fishing charters, or directions to local antiques stores and museums. The inn maintains a fleet of sturdy bicycles, and the staff is always prepared with maps and suggestions about touring routes that reveal the beauties of the area. The kitchen offers a picnic basket menu so guests can take a bit of the Inn's fine cuisine with them when they head out into the Maine waters or countryside.

An Excellent Table

Kennebunkport's summer residents, who were called "rusticators" by the locals, sought not only healthy activities but also healthful foods that combined farm-fresh produce and local seafood and game with the sophistication of urban dining. A summer menu from one of the seaside hotels offers five courses, including such seasonal delights as "Broiled Salmon Steak [with] lemon butter," "Summer Squash," and "Blueberry Pie." "As there is a farm connected with the house," this hotel informed prospective clients, "we raise our own Vegetables, and take them as needed, fresh and of the best. Also, our Milk, Butter and Eggs are from the Farm."

Although nowadays produce grown directly on the property of the White Barn Inn is limited to fresh herbs, chef Jonathan Cartwright has sought out local foragers who bring freshly gathered mushrooms, fiddlehead ferns, and wild blueberries to the kitchen in season every day. Lobsters, diver-harvested sea scallops,

Coach and Buckboard to take large parties out on excursions." Facilities were developed for the newly popular sports of tennis and golf, including a score of tennis courts and three golf courses. Canoeing and sailing were common pursuits, along with sea bathing and fishing. Traditionalists enjoyed carriage outings that terminated in lavish picnics. By 1900, with the advent of an electric trolley, adventurous summer residents added "trolley tripping" to their amusements, bustling up and down the shore to attend a full schedule of dances and musical programs.

To keep today's guests amused, the manager of the White Barn Inn prepares a daily note that appears in each guest's room, including a weather forecast along and just-caught tuna, salmon, and striped sea bass are purchased directly from fishermen who daily ply the cold Maine waters. Local game, including guinea hens, turkey, and venison, garnished with wild mushrooms, New England cranberries, and preserved Maine blueberries, appear seasonally on the restaurant's ever-changing menu. A cheese board features artisanal selections from New England and European dairies.

While these ingredients reflect the changing seasons of Maine and surrounding New England, the sophisticated recipes at the White Barn Inn reveal the artistry of a European-trained chef who delights in combining classic preparations with contemporary creativity. A lobster spring roll featuring moist meat and julienned Asian vegetables bound in a golden fried wrapper is an ingenious hybrid of the traditional Maine lobster roll and a Thai spring roll. A grilled tournedo of local cod with spring pea purée, fried shrimp, and potato sticks combines local ingredients in a preparation that playfully recalls that English seaside favorite, fish and chips. A winter entrée of grilled venison

sauced with port and Madeira and served with a potato custard timbale incorporates traditional European and New England flavors in a stunning new way.

DAYS OF GRACE AND LEISURE

The advent of the automobile significantly changed the way people summered in America. While the railroad was the traditional mode of travel, families were likely to relocate for weeks and months at a time at a single destination, living in seasonal cottages or taking rooms for long stays at large hotels. Once the automobile gained in popularity, summer vacationers were more mobile and less likely to stay for long in one holiday destination. As train travel dwindled and automobiles replaced both the newfangled trolley and the old-fashioned carriage, the pace of life sped up even more. Many of the large hotels lost much of their clientele and closed their doors.

Still, tourists, artists, and writers came to savor Kennebunkport's natural beauty and historic architecture. In 1927 a watercolor of a Federal-style doorway by Abbot Graves, an artist who frequented Kennebunkport, graced the cover of a summer issue of The Literary Digest. "It . . . might be anywhere in the old comfortable New England towns where Colonial architecture still abounds and is cared for," notes the magazine's editor. "It reminds us of the days of grace and leisure that have in recent years slipped away."

there are the stone-walled pastures that early summer powders cheerily with buttercups and daisies."

For those who belong to what one of the area's first developers described as "the most fastidious class of patronage"—travelers who seek unspoiled nature, a region filled with history and culture, luxurious accommodations, and gourmet cuisine—Kennebunkport remains an ideal destination. The White Barn Inn beautifully expresses the unique regional character of old Maine style, providing the perfect setting from which to explore the region in every season and to savor the best, freshest products from the surrounding land and sea.

SEASONAL
NEW ENGLAND CUISINE

The coast of Maine is a mercurial place, full of moods and marvelous surprises. Every few months the region reveals a different side of itself: the tender warmth and bounty of spring; the bright, exuberant days of summer; the mellow, mysterious shades of autumn; and the

Somehow, Kennebunkport and the surrounding coastal region possesses an uncanny ability to transcend time, retaining its rugged land and seascapes, protecting its elegant architecture, and still appealing to the world-weary visitor. This description of Kennebunkport from a 1930 novel by Booth Tarkington still perfectly describes the seaside town: "Away from the tumbled coast and the rocky woodland of pine and juniper, the village itself, like some outpost wandered into alien country, wears the very aspect of . . . old New England. There are little streets of clean white green-shuttered houses as old as the great wine-glass elms that dip shadows down upon the roofs; there are two white churches with columned porticoes and Christopher Wrenn steeples, and, for the landward borders,

alternately tempestuous and serenely silent winter. Each season has its own activities: long bicycle rides, beach picnics, hikes beneath the changing leaves, sleigh rides, and chestnut roasting parties. Each has its particular bounty from the waters, sky, and earth: lobsters, tuna, clams, and salmon; quail, pheasant, venison, and lamb; baby greens, mushrooms, berries, and apples. Each has its own comforts, whether bundling up by the fire, enjoying cool breezes on the beach, or swimming in the ocean or a woodland pool. And each has its own appetites: spring's taste for bright, green flavors; summer's desire for cooling soups and light, fresh dishes; autumn's pleasure in rich colors, textures, and tastes; and winter's hunger for savory stews and roasted game. At the White Barn Inn, every offering on the menu rep-

resents a perfect marriage of the freshest local ingredients with the spirit of the season.

The exquisite dishes created by the White Barn Inn's executive chef celebrate these seasonal elements in imaginative and deeply satisfying presentations. Seared scallops harvested by divers from Maine's icy waters and garnished with caviar, fresh asparagus, and a light foam of champagne sauce capture the colors, scents, and tastes of spring in Kennebunkport. A plate of strawberry shortcake, with towering layers of pale golden cake and juicy red strawberries and topped with a puffy cloud of cream, celebrates the uncomplicated pleasures of summer. A Thanksgiving dinner of roasted turkey garnished with cranberry-port compote recalls the autumnal largesse of Maine's forests, alive with wild game, colorful leaves, and berries. And a midwinter dinner of savory venison drizzled with Madeira sauce and studded with preserved blueberries provides the perfect antidote to the icy, white world that glistens beyond the inn's windows and doors.

The alchemist behind these vibrant pairings of seasonal ingredients is Jonathan Cartwright, an internationally trained chef who brings his love of European cuisine and passion for the offerings of New England's land and sea to his work. It is his goal to find the freshest local ingredients and to cook them in a style that blends a classic European approach with a contemporary attitude infused with imagination and the desire to delight and surprise even the most jaded palate. The result is a perfect balance of elegance and simplicity with just a hint of whimsy that enhances the essence of

cook can continue to enjoy the White Barn Inn experience at home by re-creating their favorite formal meals for friends or exploring the chef's suggestions for more relaxed offerings to be enjoyed in seasonal outdoor meals. Even though some of the special New England ingredients featured in these pages may be unavailable in certain parts of the country, the lessons shared here will inspire home chefs to begin experimenting more creatively with the local ingredients at hand. And many of the tips about cooking and entertaining that come from this Relais Gourmand kitchen can help any host transform a dinner party at home into an extraordinary, unforgettable meal. Share these menus with those you love and invite them to join in this celebration of sophisticated seasonal cuisine.

each season's offerings. While the chef creates intricate pairings of sauces and garnishes for the tables of the White Barn Inn, he never loses sight of the pure joy that can be found in preparing an easy, flavorful meal at home or for an informal outing. Cooking should not be too serious, he believes, because that takes all the fun out of it.

The menus and recipes that follow explore the full spectrum of the chef's genius and passion for seasonal cuisine. No true lover of food will want to miss the dramatic delights of dining at the White Barn Inn's restaurant, where attentive waiters deliver course after course with professional precision and, upon request, pair each perfectly with vintages chosen from an expertly selected, extensive wine cellar. But those who love to

Spring at the
WHITE BARN INN

S pring comes late to Maine, often not breaking free from winter's grip until the last few days of May. In Kennebunkport a gloriously patriotic Memorial Day parade heralds the official opening of the season. Although the parade route is short—just down the hill from the fire station on Temple Street, through Dock Square, over the bridge that spans the Kennebunk River, and back again—there is plenty of time for old-fashioned American flag waving, horn blowing, drum rolling, baton twirling, and speechifying— sometimes even featuring the heartfelt words of former President George H. Bush, a long-time summer resident of Kennebunkport. Children, teenage music makers, grown-up bagpipers, veterans, firefighters, and police officers all join the throng, honoring the heroes of bygone wars and basking in the long-awaited springtime warmth.

The earth finally thaws and brightly colored bulbs of crocus, narcissus, and daffodil work their way up to the sun. Cherry trees blossom with silent explosions of white, pale pink, and dark rose petals. Lilacs bristle with short-lived clusters in shades of lavender and deep violet. Lawns receive the first mowing of the year, filling the air with a vivid green perfume. Wild rose bushes that form a tangled hedge along the rocky coast bloom with citrus-scented flowers of pale pink and yellow. Seasonal residents and weekenders flock to Kennebunkport during the first weeks of spring, seeking the pleasures of fresh sea air, a colorful landscape, and a quaint New England village. The rooms of the White Barn Inn are booked well in advance, and the dining room tables are full.

Chef Jonathan Cartwright anticipates spring with pleasure, welcoming the arrival of fresh, local produce that transforms winter's menu into something altogether new. After months of preparing hearty ragouts and savory soups, he delights in concocting spring dishes packed with color and lighter, brighter tastes. Foragers arrive at the kitchen's back door bringing the first growth of fiddlehead ferns and forest mushrooms, and growers deliver tender chives, baby spinach, crisp watercress, and tart rhubarb, which they have coaxed into early harvest in local greenhouses. On the Kennebunkport docks, fishermen revel in the season's catch, especially delicately flavored salmon, buttery cod, and the last diver-harvested scallops. Lobsters are plentiful and spring lamb is right on time.

In keeping with the season, the White Barn Inn's appetizer menu features watercress soup garnished with

get outside and enjoy the spring air, so they offer a menu of picnic food that can be packed into hampers or backpacks and eaten outdoors. Offerings like cold grilled salmon, paired with an asparagus salad, provide light and flavorful refreshment for an alfresco lunch.

The following recipes provide a sampling of spring's culinary pleasures at the White Barn Inn. In the spirit of the season, you might want to invite friends over for a springtime feast and prepare one of the formal dinners featuring young lamb or a selection of seafood. By

Offerings like cold grilled salmon, paired with an asparagus salad, offer light and flavorful refreshment for an alfresco lunch.

a lobster tail, spring greens dressed with an aged balsamic vinaigrette, and a lobster spring roll, one of the chef's signature creations. Grilled guinea hen on creamed spinach with spring peas and a woodland mushroom sauce, an entrée, brings together the essences of spring's first earthy breath with tender green things. A rhubarb crêpe soufflé served with buttermilk ice cream marries the tart and sweet flavors of the season.

A formal, five-course meal is just one of the pleasures to be enjoyed during this season. The staff at the White Barn Inn understands that guests also want to

preparing a few ingredients in advance and buying time—serving a chilled soup, prepared hours earlier, between courses, for example—home cooks can host a memorable evening that captures the bounty of the table at the White Barn Inn while still enjoying their own party. A simpler picnic lunch menu offers great rewards of pure spring flavors and colors with limited effort. And although the breakfast of poached eggs on lobster hash requires cooks to make a batch of lobster bisque in advance, it is easily assembled and promises to delight.

SPRING MENUS

A Spring Celebration at the White Barn Inn

Carpaccio of Aged Tenderloin
with a Szechuan Pepper and Soy Vinaigrette on
a Salad of Beets and Daikon Radish

Hollandaise-Glazed Local Halibut on Spring Fiddleheads
and Forest Mushrooms

Iced Cantaloupe and Lychee Soup

Herb-Roasted Spring Lamb with Tomato Chardonnay Sauce on Ratatouille
and Pesto Potato Purée

or

Grilled Breast of Guinea Hen on Creamed Spinach
with Potatoes, Spring Peas, and a Woodland Mushroom Sauce

Lemon Balm Soufflé and Rosewater Ice Cream

A Springtime Picnic

Rhubarb Smoothies

Grilled Salmon with Spring Fiddleheads, Asparagus, and Scallions

A Selection of Cheeses with Red Currant Chutney

·

A Spring Cocktail

Stars and Stripes

·

A Spring Seafood Menu

Diver-Harvested Scallops on Asparagus with Champagne Foam and Caviar

Lobster Spring Roll with Carrot, Daikon Radish, and Snow Peas
in a Thai-Inspired Spicy Sweet Sauce

Kalamansi Sour Lemon Sorbet

Grilled Tournedos of Local Cod Loin with Crispy Shrimp and
Calamari on a Spring Pea Purée with a Piquant Sauce

"Twice-Baked" Rhubarb Crêpe Soufflé with Buttermilk Ice Cream

·

Breakfast by the Pool

Breakfast Fruit Bowl

Poached Eggs on Kennebunkport Lobster Hash

Freshly Baked Muffins

A Spring Celebration at The White Barn Inn

Dinner at the White Barn Inn begins with an amuse bouche—a beautifully garnished, bite-size serving of something the chef dreamed up that day to "amuse the mouth" and tease the appetite. Try serving one of these diminutive dishes at a dinner party at home. It's a nice way to please your guests, while affording yourself an extra five minutes in the kitchen to finish assembling the appetizer course below.

CARPACCIO OF AGED TENDERLOIN WITH A SZECHUAN PEPPER AND SOY VINAIGRETTE ON A SALAD OF BEETS AND DAIKON RADISH

In the White Barn Inn's professionally equipped kitchen, the chef uses a slicing machine that makes it easy to carve paper-thin slices from the beef tenderloin. When preparing this at home, just use a very sharp knife and slice the beef, partially frozen for about one hour, as thinly as possible, at least ¼ inch thick. If desired, you can cover the slices with waxed paper and pound them more thinly using a meat mallet.

Serves 4

1 teaspoon ground Szechuan red pepper

½ teaspoon cayenne pepper

1 pinch freshly ground white pepper

½ teaspoon paprika

1 pinch salt

10 ounces center cut beef tenderloin,
in one piece

1 tablespoon olive oil

Szechuan Pepper and Soy Vinaigrette (see page 24)

Salad of Beets and Daikon Radish (see page 25)

In a small bowl, combine the Szechuan, cayenne, and white peppers, paprika, and salt. Spread on a clean cutting board.

Roll the tenderloin in the spice mixture until evenly covered.

In a large skillet, heat the olive oil over high heat. When the oil is hot, add the beef and sear for a few seconds on each side, just long enough to brown the outside of the meat and seal the spice crust.

Place the seared beef on a large plate, cover with plastic wrap, and chill in the freezer for 1 hour.

Using a very sharp knife, slice the beef into paper-thin slices, cutting across the grain. Arrange the slices on four serving plates. Drizzle with the Szechuan Pepper and Soy Vinaigrette and surround with Salad of Beets and Daikon Radish.

SZECHUAN PEPPER AND SOY VINAIGRETTE

Makes about ½ cup

2 tablespoons soy sauce

4 tablespoons blended oil (see Note)

1 teaspoon sherry vinegar

1 teaspoon ground Szechuan red pepper

Salt and freshly ground pepper

Combine the soy sauce, oil, vinegar, and Szechuan pepper in a small bowl. Blend thoroughly, using a hand-held blender or wire whisk. Season the dressing with salt and pepper to taste.

Note: Blended oil is a mixture of 90 percent vegetable oil and 10 percent olive oil.

SALAD OF BEETS AND DAIKON RADISH

Serves 4

½ pound red beets, peeled

½ pound daikon radish, peeled

1 tablespoon soy sauce

2 tablespoons blended oil (see Note)

1 teaspoon chopped fresh cilantro

Salt and freshly ground pepper

Using a mandoline or a Japanese vegetable slicer, cut the beets and the daikon radish into thin slices, then cut the slices into a fine julienne.

Using a whisk or a hand-held blender, whisk the soy sauce and the oil until the mixture is slightly thickened and forms an emulsion. Add the cilantro and mix well. Season to taste with salt and pepper.

Just before serving, combine the beet and the daikon radish in a large bowl and toss with the dressing.

Note: Blended oil is a mixture of 90 percent vegetable oil and 10 percent olive oil.

Hollandaise-Glazed Local Halibut
on Spring Fiddleheads and Forest Mushrooms

*North Atlantic halibut is a firm-textured fish with a mild flavor that perfectly comple-
ments the fiddleheads and mushrooms. Glazing the hollandaise by running the
just-sauced fish under a hot broiler gives this dish an appealing texture and appearance. It also prevents the sauce from dripping down the sides of the fish onto the
vegetables that surround it. Fiddleheads and forest mushrooms have such nice flavor
that they can stand on their own and don't need much sauce.*

Serves 4

HOLLANDAISE

½ cup full-bodied white wine, such as chardonnay

½ cup champagne vinegar

1 teaspoon cracked black peppercorns

1 sprig fresh parsley

1 shallot, finely chopped

4 egg yolks

½ pound (2 sticks) unsalted butter, melted

1 teaspoon chopped fresh parsley

HALIBUT AND VEGETABLES

1 cup fiddlehead ferns

1 tablespoon blended oil (see Note)

1½ pounds North Atlantic halibut filet, cut into four pieces

Salt and freshly ground white pepper

2 teaspoons unsalted butter

1 shallot, finely chopped

½ cup chanterelle or other wild mushrooms,
lightly rinsed, drained, and towel dried

¼ cup Parsley Oil (see page 29)

For the hollandaise: Combine the wine, vinegar, peppercorns, parsley, and shallots in a medium saucepan. Bring to a boil over high heat, then lower the heat and cook until the mixture is reduced by half, about 5 minutes. Strain through a fine sieve, discarding the shallots and peppercorns, and reserve the liquid reduction.

Place a heat-resistant mixing bowl over a pan of boiling water. Add the egg yolks and ⅜ cup of the hollandaise reduction and whisk until the mixture doubles in volume and turns pale yellow. At this stage, the whisk should leave a distinct trail when passed through the sauce. Remove the mixing bowl from the pan of water and gradually add the melted butter, whisking continuously. The finished hollandaise should have the consistency of ketchup. If it is too thick, add some of the reserved reduction to thin it. Season to taste with salt and pepper, and stir in the chopped parsley. Keep the hollandaise in a warm place (but do not set the pan on a stove burner) until ready to serve.

To prepare the vegetables: bring a medium saucepan filled with salted water to a boil. Rinse the fiddlehead ferns, add them to the pan, and blanch for 1 minute, or until tender but still bright green. Remove with a sieve or slotted spoon and refresh in a large bowl of ice water until cool, then drain.

Place the oil in a large skillet over high heat. Season the halibut filets with salt and freshly ground white pepper and place them in the hot oil, searing for 1 minute before reducing the heat to medium. Add 1 teaspoon of butter to the pan and continue cooking the filets for 3 to 4 minutes, or until golden brown on one side. Turn the filets and cook for 5 minutes longer, until cooked through. The thickness of the filets will determine the exact cooking time. The goal is to have a golden brown exterior with a moist center.

Melt the remaining teaspoon of butter in a large sauté pan over high heat. Add the chopped shallot and sauté until translucent but not browned. Add the mushrooms and cook over high heat for 3 minutes, tossing occasionally. Stir in the fiddlehead ferns and season to taste with salt and pepper.

To serve, preheat the broiler. If four shallow, heat-resistant serving bowls are available, divide the fiddlehead and mushroom mixture among them. Place a halibut filet on top of each serving and cover it with hollandaise. Run the bowls under a hot broiler for a few seconds, until the hollandaise turns golden brown. Alternatively, place the halibut filets on a baking sheet, cover each filet with hollandaise, and run the baking sheet under the broiler, just until the hollandaise turns golden brown. Arrange the glazed filets in four shallow bowls on top of the fiddlehead and mushroom mixture. Drizzle with Parsley Oil and serve.

Note: Blended oil is a mixture of 90 percent vegetable oil and 10 percent olive oil.

FIDDLEHEAD FERNS

IN SPRING THE FOREST FLOOR IS COVERED WITH BABY FERNS SHAPED
LIKE THE HEAD OF A FIDDLE. FIDDLEHEAD FERNS HAVE A UNIQUE FLAVOR THAT COMBINES
THE FRESH GREEN TASTE OF ASPARAGUS WITH THE RICHER NOTES OF ARTICHOKE.

PARSLEY OIL

Makes 1 cup

1 bunch fresh parsley

1 cup blended oil (see Note)

Fill a medium saucepan with water and bring it to a boil. Drop the parsley into the boiling water for a few seconds, then drain and refresh in a large bowl of ice water until cool.

Squeeze all excess liquid from the blanched parsley and place it in the jar of a blender with the oil. Blend the mixture on high for 30 seconds, until the parsley is pureed. Strain the oil through a fine sieve lined with cheesecloth. Store any remaining parsley oil in a covered container in the refrigerator.

Note: Blended oil is a mixture of 90 percent vegetable oil and 10 percent olive oil.

Iced Cantaloupe and Lychee Soup

This chilled soup has such a delicious melony fragrance,
your guests will be tempted to take time out from eating simply to sit
and smell it. But encourage them to eat this soup
while it's still icy cold, as it provides a refreshing contrast
to the herbed lamb dish that follows. If you can't find fresh lychees,
frozen or canned lychees can be substituted.

Serves 4

2 cups peeled, diced cantaloupe

1 cup peeled and pitted fresh lychees

1 cup white dessert wine, such as muscat

1 cup champagne, chilled

In the jar of a blender, combine the cantaloupe, lychees, and dessert wine. Purée, working in batches if necessary, until completely smooth.

Strain the puréed fruit mixture through a fine sieve into a stainless steel or glass pitcher and chill until ready to serve. Just before serving, gently stir the chilled champagne into the fruit mixture. Divide among four soup bowls and serve.

HERB-ROASTED SPRING LAMB
WITH TOMATO CHARDONNAY SAUCE
ON RATATOUILLE AND PESTO POTATO PURÉE

Because this dish has several components—the roasted lamb,
a sauce flavored with two different reduced meat stocks (or jus, as reduced stocks
are called in a French kitchen), and two vegetable accompaniments—it does require
advance planning. The stocks can be made days ahead of time and refrigerated
(or even weeks in advance and frozen) until you are ready to make the sauce.
The pesto will also keep for several days properly stored and refrigerated,
and the ratatouille actually tastes best if made a day before serving. Have your butcher
french the rack of lamb by scraping away any meat and fat from the upper portion
of the bones. The final presentation is so full of intense flavor and color that you
and your guests will find it well worth the advance effort.

Serves 4

1 cup plain dried bread crumbs

2 tablespoons mixed dried herbs (rosemary, parsley,
chervil, and tarragon)

2 pounds lamb rump, trimmed of all fat

1½ pounds rack of lamb, frenched

Salt and freshly ground pepper

2 tablespoons unsalted butter

2 teaspoons Dijon mustard

2 cups Ratatouille (see page 34)

1½ cups Pesto Potato Purée (see page 35)

4 red baby bell peppers,
roasted, peeled, seeded, and halved

1 cup Tomato Chardonnay Sauce (see page 37)

4 Herb Chips, for garnish (see page 38)

Preheat the oven to 350°F.

Combine the bread crumbs and dried herbs in the bowl of a food processor and pulse until very finely chopped. Pass this mixture through a medium sieve set over a large bowl to remove any large pieces.

Season the lamb rump and rack of lamb with salt and pepper. Heat a large, heavy skillet over high heat and add 1 tablespoon butter. Working with one piece of lamb at a time, sear the meat in the hot pan, turning so that all sides are lightly browned. Spread the mustard on the back of the lamb rack and roll it in the herb-and-bread crumb mixture until evenly coated.

Place both pieces of lamb on a rack inside a baking pan and roast for about 10 minutes, or until a meat thermometer placed in the center of the lamb rack reads 110°F for medium rare or 140° for medium. Allow the lamb to rest in a warm place for 10 minutes before carving. Just before serving, cut the lamb rack into four equal portions and slice the rump into medallions.

To serve, place ½ cup of the Ratatouille in the center of each plate. Using two teaspoons, shape heaped spoonfuls of the hot Pesto Potato Purée into eight ovals, rounded on top and bottom, and place one inside each roasted red pepper half. Place two stuffed pepper halves on each plate. Arrange the individual portions of carved lamb on top of the Ratatouille. Whisk the remaining tablespoon of butter into the Tomato Chardonnay Sauce and drizzle 1 to 2 tablespoons over each serving of the lamb. Garnish each plate with an Herb Chip.

Ratatouille

This classic Provençal dish
of gently cooked vegetables improves in flavor
when made a day in advance.

Makes 4 cups

1 medium eggplant, peeled

1 medium zucchini

1 medium yellow squash

1 red bell pepper

1 yellow bell pepper

1 yellow onion

1 clove garlic

¼ cup olive oil

½ cup V-8 juice

Salt and freshly ground pepper

Cut the eggplant, zucchini, yellow squash, red pepper, and yellow pepper into ¼-inch dice, keeping each ingredient separate. Mince the onion and garlic.

Heat the olive oil in a large skillet over medium heat. Add the onion and garlic and cook for 3 minutes, until transparent but not brown.

Increase the heat to medium high and add the peppers, yellow squash, zucchini, and eggplant at 1-minute intervals, stirring continuously. Once all the ingredients have been added, cook the vegetable mixture 5 minutes longer.

Add the V-8 juice and cook over medium high heat for 5 minutes longer. Season to taste with salt and pepper.

PESTO POTATO PURÉE

Makes about 2 cups

½ pound Idaho potatoes, peeled and cut into rough dice

¼ cup olive oil

4 tablespoons (½ stick) unsalted butter

2 tablespoons Pesto (see page 36)

Fill a medium saucepan with salted water and bring to a boil. Add the potatoes and cook for 10 to 15 minutes, until easily pierced by a fork. Drain and place in a large bowl. Add the olive oil and butter, and mash just until the lumps disappear. Avoid overmashing the potatoes, which will release starches and make them gooey.

Cover the puréed potatoes and keep in a warm place while preparing the rest of the meal. Just before serving, add the Pesto and mix well.

A SENIOR MEMBER OF THE HOUSEKEEPING STAFF MAKES HER ROUNDS
TO KEEP PILLOWS PLUMPED, COVERS SMOOTHED, FLOWERS FRESH, AND EVERY DETAIL
CAREFULLY REVIEWED FOR THE COMFORT AND CONVENIENCE OF GUESTS.

PESTO

*Properly stored, pesto will keep without changing color
for several days. Transfer the finished pesto to a nonreactive glass
or stainless steel container. Pour a thin layer of olive oil
over the pesto and cover the container with aluminum
foil to keep out light and air.*

Makes about 1½ cups

1 bunch fresh basil leaves

½ bunch fresh flat leaf parsley

1 clove garlic

¾ cup freshly grated
Parmesan cheese

1 cup olive oil

¼ cup shelled pistachios

¼ cup pine nuts

¼ cup shelled walnuts

Salt and freshly ground pepper

Combine the basil, parsley, garlic, cheese, and olive oil in the bowl of a food processor and pulse until finely chopped.

Add the nuts and chop for a few more seconds, being careful not to overprocess the mixture. The nuts should be chopped to a medium texture but not finely ground.

Season the pesto with salt and pepper to taste. Refrigerate until ready to use.

TOMATO CHARDONNAY SAUCE

*Before mixed vegetable juices such as V-8 juice were commercially available,
cooks often used tomato purée to add flavor and texture to stocks and
sauces. Chef Cartwright likes to use mixed vegetable juice instead, because
it has a milder flavor than tomato purée. Another common addition
to the stockpot is mirepoix, a mixture of sautéed aromatic vegetables.
V-8 juice serves as a kind of instant mirepoix.*

Makes about 1½ cups

1 tablespoon unsalted butter

1 medium onion, diced

2 medium tomatoes, diced

6 sprigs fresh basil

6 sprigs fresh parsley

1 cup chardonnay
(or other full-bodied white wine)

1 cup V-8 juice

1 cup Veal Jus (see page 68)

1 cup Lamb Jus (see page 68)

Salt and freshly ground pepper

In a medium saucepan with a heavy bottom, melt the butter over medium high
heat. Add the onions, tomatoes, basil, and parsley and sauté for 3 to 4 minutes, until
the onions are transparent but not brown and the tomatoes begin to break down.

Add the chardonnay and cook over high heat until the mixture is reduced by
half. Add the V-8 juice, Veal Jus, and Lamb Jus, and continue cooking over high
heat until the mixture is slightly reduced, about 5 minutes.

Reduce the heat to medium low and simmer the sauce for 30 minutes. Strain
through a fine sieve and season with salt and pepper to taste.

HERB CHIPS

If you don't have Silpat nonstick baking mats,
you can make these herb chips by placing the potato slices on a nonstick
baking sheet or a regular baking sheet coated with vegetable spray.
Then cover them during baking with a glass baking dish.

Makes 4

1 large Idaho potato, peeled

4 sprigs fresh flat-leaf parsley or fresh chervil

Preheat the oven to 300° F.

Cut the potato into wafer-thin slices using a mandoline or a Japanese vegetable slicer. Reserve the eight largest slices and discard the rest.

Place a Silpat mat on a baking sheet. Place four potato slices on the mat. Lay a small herb sprig in the center of each potato slice. Top with another potato slice to form four "sandwiches," aligning the edges of the potato slices as closely as possible. Cover the potato slices with another Silpat mat.

Bake the chips for 5 to 10 minutes, until golden brown and crisp.

GRILLED BREAST OF GUINEA HEN
ON CREAMED SPINACH WITH POTATOES, SPRING PEAS,
AND A WOODLAND MUSHROOM SAUCE

*This is a lovely spring-flavored game recipe that you can substitute
for the entrée in either of the formal menus in this section.
While many Americans don't like to eat heavier-tasting game birds,
they tend to love the light, savory meat of guinea hen, which tastes like
a very flavorful chicken. If you can't find guinea hens,
substitute free-range chicken.*

Serves 4

5 tablespoons unsalted butter

1 cup chanterelles or other wild mushrooms,
rinsed, drained, and towel dried

1 cup full-bodied white wine such as chardonnay

2 cups Guinea Hen Jus (see page 42)

1 tablespoon chopped shallots

1 pound fresh spinach, stemmed, washed, and drained

½ pound shelled English peas

½ pound shelled fava beans

12 new potatoes or small white potatoes, peeled

1 cup heavy cream

4 split guinea hen breasts, boned, with wing attached and skin on

Salt and freshly ground pepper

In a medium sauté pan, melt 1 tablespoon of butter over medium high heat. Add
the mushrooms and sauté for 2 minutes. Stir in the white wine. Remove the mushrooms with a slotted spoon and reserve. Increase the heat to high and boil until the
wine has almost completely evaporated. Add the Guinea Hen Jus and return to a
boil. Continue cooking over high heat until the sauce reduces and thickens enough
to coat the back of a spoon. Remove from the heat.

In a large sauté pan, melt 1 tablespoon of butter. Add the chopped shallots and sauté until soft and transparent. Add the spinach and cook for 1 minute, tossing until it is wilted and tender. Transfer the spinach to a sieve and press it to remove any excess liquid.

Bring 4 cups of water to a boil in a large saucepan. Add the peas and the fava beans and blanch for 2 minutes. Drain and rinse immediately with cold water. Remove the skins from the fava beans.

Preheat the oven to 400°F.

In a shallow ovenproof casserole large enough to hold the hen breasts and the potatoes, melt 2 tablespoons of butter over medium high heat. Add the peeled potatoes and turn to coat with butter. Place the casserole in the oven and bake for 15 minutes, or until the potatoes are easily pierced by a fork.

Pour the cream into a medium saucepan with a heavy bottom. Bring to a boil over medium high heat, then reduce the heat and simmer until the cream is reduced by half. Combine the reduced cream and the spinach in the bowl of a food processor and pulse several times to form a purée. Season to taste with salt and pepper.

Preheat a gas or charcoal grill. Grill the hen breasts for 3 minutes on each side, until lightly browned but not cooked through. Reduce the oven temperature to 350°F.

Transfer the guinea hen breasts to the center of the casserole with the potatoes. Surround with the potatoes. Place the casserole in the oven and bake for 8 minutes, until the juices run clear.

While the hen breasts are in the oven, warm the spinach purée in a medium saucepan with a heavy bottom. Melt the remaining tablespoon of butter in a large sauté pan over medium low heat and add the blanched English peas and fava beans, tossing just to warm through. Season to taste with salt and pepper. Return the mushrooms to the reduced sauce and warm over low heat.

To serve, spoon a portion of spinach purée in the center of each plate. Place a hen breast on top of the spinach. Divide the peas, fava beans, and potatoes into four portions, placing them around the edge of each plate. Spoon the mushroom sauce over the hen breasts and potatoes and serve.

Guinea Hen Jus

*The exact proportions of vegetables and herbs are not what matters
in this stock recipe. Just use what you've got on hand
to create a well-balanced flavor.*

Makes 3 cups

4 pounds guinea hen bones or chicken bones

½ pound (about 1 cup) diced mixed aromatic vegetables,
such as carrots, leeks, onions, and celery

1 clove garlic, crushed

12 sprigs fresh herbs, such as thyme, rosemary, and tarragon

1 cup dry, fruity white wine, such as sauvignon blanc

Preheat the oven to 450°F.

Place the bones in a large roasting pan and roast, turning occasionally, for 15 minutes, until golden brown. Add the vegetables to the pan and continue roasting for 5 minutes.

Transfer the bones and vegetables to a large stockpot and add the garlic, herbs, and white wine. Cover with water and bring to a boil over high heat, skimming off any scum that rises to the surface. Reduce the heat to medium and simmer the stock for 4 hours, until reduced by half.

Strain the stock through a fine sieve into a clean saucepan. Bring to a boil over medium high heat, then reduce the heat to medium and cook until reduced by half. The finished jus will have the consistency of a lightweight sauce.

Reserve 2 cups of jus for the Woodland Mushroom Sauce and freeze the remainder in ice cube trays. When frozen, transfer the cubes of stock to zipper-lock bags and store in the freezer for future use.

Lemon Balm Soufflé and Rosewater Ice Cream

*There's a myth that soufflés are difficult to make. They're actually quite simple
as long as you follow the recipe carefully. Timing is important, too.
The uncooked soufflés can stand on the kitchen counter for up to 30 minutes before
you bake them. Just put them in the preheated oven 15 minutes before you
want to serve dessert, and they'll come out perfectly.*

Serves 8

SOUFFLÉ BASE

2 cups milk

¾ cup sugar

8 to 10 sprigs fresh lemon balm

3 egg yolks

½ cup crème patissière powder
(or ¼ cup all-purpose flour sifted with ¼ cup cornstarch)

Combine the milk, half the sugar, and the lemon balm in a medium saucepan with
a heavy bottom. Bring to a boil over medium high heat, then transfer the mixture
to a nonreactive glass or stainless steel storage container and let cool to room temperature. Cover and refrigerate for 24 hours to allow the flavor to develop fully.

Strain the infused milk mixture through a sieve into a clean saucepan. Bring to
a boil over medium high heat, then immediately remove from the heat.

In a large bowl, beat the egg yolks until smooth. Beat in the remaining sugar and
the crème patissière powder (or flour-and-cornstarch mixture).

Add a few tablespoons of the hot milk mixture to the egg yolk mixture and beat
until combined. Beat in a few more tablespoons, and repeat this step once more to
bring the egg mixture gradually to the temperature of the hot milk mixture without
curdling the eggs.

Slowly add the warmed egg mixture to the hot milk, whisking constantly. Cook
over low heat, whisking constantly, until the mixture is thick enough to coat the
back of a spoon. Let cool to room temperature.

SOUFFLÉ

2 tablespoons unsalted butter

3½ tablespoons sugar, plus additional for dusting

4 egg yolks

½ cup limoncello,
or other lemon-flavored liqueur

Soufflé Base (see page 43)

8 egg whites

Preheat the oven to 375°F. Butter eight ramekins (3½ inches in diameter, 1½ inches deep) and dust them with a small amount of sugar, shaking out any excess.

In a large bowl, combine the egg yolks and limoncello, and beat until the mixture is foamy and light in color. Add the Soufflé Base and stir vigorously.

In another large bowl, combine the egg whites with the sugar. Using an electric mixer, beat the mixture until it forms soft peaks. Carefully fold the beaten egg whites into the soufflé base mixture.

Fill the ramekins with the mixture and place them on a rack in the center of the oven. Bake for 15 minutes, or until golden and puffed.

Serve immediately. At the table, break a hole in the center of each soufflé and pour in a small amount of Lemon Sauce (see page 46).

LEMON SAUCE

Makes 2 cups

1 cup sugar

½ cup fresh lemon juice

5½ tablespoons limoncello or
other lemon-flavored liqueur

In a medium saucepan with a heavy bottom, combine the sugar and 1 cup of water. Bring to a boil over high heat, and continue to cook until the mixture caramelizes into a light golden brown syrup.

Remove from the heat and add the lemon juice. Return to medium heat, and whisk the syrup until the lemon juice is thoroughly incorporated.

Remove the syrup from the heat and whisk in the limoncello. Let cool to room temperature. The sauce will keep, covered and refrigerated, for two weeks.

ADVANCE PREPARATION IS THE KEY TO SUCCESS IN
A PROFESSIONAL KITCHEN WHERE AS MANY AS 15 COOKS WORK
TOGETHER THROUGHOUT THE DAY TO PREPARE DINNER.
MANY RECIPES IN THIS BOOK CAN BE PARTIALLY PREPARED HOURS,
AND IN SOME CASES, EVEN A DAY IN ADVANCE,
MAKING IT EASIER FOR HOME CHEFS TO ENJOY
THEIR OWN DINNER PARTIES.

ROSEWATER ICE CREAM

*The flavor of this ice cream is wonderfully subtle and
surprising. Paired with the lemon balm soufflé,
it is reminiscent of the citrusy smell of the wild rosebushes
that grow along the waterfront in Kennebunkport.*

Makes 4 cups

2 cups heavy cream

1½ cups half-and-half

¼ cup rosewater

1 cup sugar

1 dozen egg yolks

In a medium saucepan with a heavy bottom, combine the cream, half-and-half, rosewater, and sugar. Bring to a boil over medium high heat, stirring constantly to avoid scorching the mixture on the bottom of the pan.

In a large bowl, beat the egg yolks until foamy and light yellow in color. Add a few tablespoons of the hot cream mixture to the egg yolks and beat until combined. Beat in a few more tablespoons of the hot cream and repeat this step once more to bring the egg yolk mixture to the temperature of the hot cream mixture without curdling the yolks.

Slowly add the warmed egg yolk mixture to the hot cream mixture, whisking constantly. Cook over low heat, whisking constantly, until thick enough to coat the back of a spoon.

Strain the mixture through a sieve into a large bowl to remove any lumps and refrigerate until cool.

Freeze in an ice cream machine, following the manufacturer's instructions. Serve a small scoop of the ice cream on the dessert plate next to the Lemon Balm Soufflé.

A Springtime Picnic

Grilled salmon is an elegant picnic dish that is also practical. If you are picnicking in a place with barbecue facilities, you can grill it on the spot (but be sure to keep the raw salmon on ice before you cook it). Otherwise, you can grill the salmon ahead of time and serve it cold over the vegetable salad.

RHUBARB SMOOTHIES

*Smoothies transport easily in an insulated thermal container
and make a refreshing accompaniment to an outdoor meal.*

Serves 4

2 cups Rhubarb Purée

6 tablespoons plain yogurt

2 cups milk

4 scoops rhubarb or strawberry sorbet

Working in two batches, combine all the ingredients in the jar of a
blender. Blend just until smooth.

Serve at once in chilled glasses, or if transporting for a picnic,
pour into a chilled insulated thermal container.

RHUBARB PURÉE

Makes 2 cups

3 cups diced rhubarb

6 tablespoons sugar

Combine the rhubarb, sugar, and 2 tablespoons of water in a medium saucepan. Bring the mixture to a boil over medium heat, stirring
occasionally. Reduce the heat to low and cover the pan. Cook over
low heat for 15 minutes, stirring occasionally.

Cool the mixture and purée it in a blender or food processor
until smooth. Strain the purée to remove any fibers and refrigerate
until ready to use.

Grilled Salmon with Spring Fiddleheads, Asparagus, and Scallions

The bright green flavors of fiddlehead ferns and asparagus dressed
in a very light vinaigrette really shine in this salad.
Slicing the asparagus tips in half reveals their delicate, leafy texture
and provides more surface for the dressing to cling to.

Serves 4

1 cup fiddlehead ferns

1 bunch scallions

1 bunch medium asparagus,
woody ends trimmed

1 ripe tomato

1 teaspoon grainy mustard

¼ cup champagne vinegar

½ cup olive oil

Salt and freshly ground pepper

2 sprigs fresh chervil

1 pound center-cut salmon filet,
cut into four pieces

Preheat a gas or charcoal grill.

Rinse and drain the fiddlehead ferns. Slice the scallions on the diagonal into ¼-inch pieces. Cut the asparagus spears on the diagonal into ½-inch pieces. Seed the tomato and cut it into fine dice.

Bring a medium saucepan filled with salted water to a boil. Add the fiddlehead ferns and blanch for 1 minute, or until tender but still bright green. Remove them with a slotted spoon and refresh them in a large bowl of ice water until cool, then drain. Repeat this step with the scallions and then with the asparagus pieces.

Place the mustard in a medium, nonreactive glas or stainless steel bowl.

Whisk in the vinegar, then gradually whisk in the oil to form an emulsion. Season the dressing to taste with salt and pepper.

Drain the fiddleheads, scallions, and asparagus and combine them in a large salad bowl with 2 tablespoons of the diced tomato. Remove the leaves from the chervil sprigs and add them to the mixture. Add enough vinaigrette to dress the salad lightly and toss, seasoning to taste with salt and pepper. Divide the salad among four serving plates.

Season the salmon filets with salt and pepper to taste. Oil the grill grate and place the filets directly over the heat. Cook for 4 minutes on each side. Arrange the grilled filets on top of the salad and serve.

FRESH FISH IS FIRMLY FLESHED AND DELICATELY SCENTED
OF THE SEA. EACH MORNING, THE CHEF OF THE WHITE BARN INN
PERSONALLY SELECTS JUST-CAUGHT SEAFOOD FROM
NEARBY DOCKS. HERE, HE FILETS WHOLE FISH TO SERVE
FOR DINNER THAT EVENING.

A Selection of Cheeses
with Red Currant Chutney

For an interesting and flavorful selection of cheeses, combine hard and creamy-textured cheeses and choose those made from a variety of milks: cow, sheep, and goat. Blue cheese makes a nice tangy addition. We use Berkshire Blue, a creamy, aged Stilton-style cheese that's especially good in summer when the cows graze on rich green grass. We also serve Bonne Bouche, a smooth, ash-ripened goat cheese made in Vermont, as well as Vermont Shepherd, a beautiful, handmade sheep's milk cheese with a rich, dry flavor, and a blue Jersey cow's milk cheese from Massachusetts. American artisanal dairies are producing some delicious cheeses, so it's worth seeking out a high-grade domestic variety made on a nearby dairy farm. Domestic cheeses can often taste better than imported ones that may have been allowed to overripen. We serve our cheese course with homemade fruit chutneys that complement the flavors of the cheese as well as satisfy the desire for something sweet at the end of the meal.

RED CURRANT CHUTNEY

Makes about 1 cup

½ cup sugar

¼ cup champagne vinegar

1 cup fresh red currants

Pinch ground ginger

Place the sugar in a medium sauté pan over medium heat and shake the pan, evenly distributing the sugar until it melts and turns into a golden brown syrup. Remove the pan from the heat and carefully add the vinegar. The mixture will bubble and "spit." When it settles, stir it gently. If some of the caramelized syrup has hardened, return the pan to the stove over medium heat and stir the mixture until the hardened bits dissolve.

Add the red currants and ginger. Cook the mixture over medium heat for 5 minutes, stirring occasionally, until some but not all of the currants break down. Remove from the heat and cool. The chutney will keep, covered and refrigerated, for up to ten days.

A Spring Cocktail

STARS AND STRIPES

*The inspiration for this cocktail comes from the red, white, and blue
striped bunting and flags hung around Kennebunkport in preparation for the Memorial
Day parade. The combination of orange-flavored vodka, tart Campari, and the sweet
citrus essence of Curaçao captures the tang of sea air on a breezy spring day.*

Makes 1 large cocktail

3½ ounces orange-flavored vodka

1 ounce Campari

½ ounce blue Curaçao

1 slice starfruit, for garnish

Mix the vodka and the Campari over ice in a shaker. Strain into a chilled martini glass.
Slowly pour the blue Curaçao into the center of the glass. It will form a blue layer float-
ing above the red layer in the bottom of the glass. Garnish with the slice of starfruit.

A Spring Seafood Menu

When people visit Kennebunkport, they usually bring an appetite for fresh seafood. This menu reveals many different flavors of the sea, from sweet scallops and lobster meat to mild, buttery cod loin. Each recipe features sauces and garnishes that complement the taste and texture of the particular seafood, offering variety throughout the meal.

DIVER-HARVESTED SCALLOPS ON ASPARAGUS WITH CHAMPAGNE FOAM AND CAVIAR

This beautiful amuse bouche perfectly captures the salty-sweet essence of the Maine coast. The champagne foam looks like the edge of a frothy wave. Diver-harvested scallops are removed by hand from the ocean bed. This method results in large, well-shaped scallops and, even more importantly, does not disturb the ocean floor.

Serves 4

2 teaspoons unsalted butter

1 shallot, diced

1 cup champagne

1 cup heavy cream

Salt, freshly ground pepper, and cayenne

Fresh lemon juice

8 asparagus spears, woody ends trimmed

1 tablespoon blended oil (see Note)

4 diver harvested scallops

1 tablespoon osetra caviar

In a medium saucepan, melt 1 teaspoon of the butter. Add the shallots and sauté for 1 minute, or until translucent but not browned. Add ¾ cup champagne to the pan and reduce the mixture by half over medium high heat. Add the cream and reduce the heat to medium. Cook the sauce until it is thick enough to coat the back of a spoon. Season to taste with salt, pepper, cayenne, and a drop or two of lemon juice.

Bring a medium saucepan of salted water to a boil. Peel the asparagus stalks and cut into 1-inch pieces. Add to the boiling water and cook just until tender but still bright green, about 2 minutes. Refresh in a large bowl of ice water until cool, then drain.

Heat the oil in a small sauté pan. Season the scallops with salt and pepper and sear in the oil for 2 minutes on each side, or until golden brown and firm to the touch.

In a clean sauté pan, melt the remaining teaspoon of butter. Add the drained asparagus and toss gently to coat with the melted butter.

Divide the asparagus among four serving plates. Place one scallop on each plate, on top of the asparagus. Top each scallop with caviar.

Reheat the sauce and add the remaining champagne. Using a hand-held blender, beat the sauce to form a light foam. Spoon the sauce over each serving, using the foamiest part of the sauce to top the scallops and caviar.

Note: Blended oil is a mixture of 90 percent vegetable oil and 10 percent olive oil.

Lobster Spring Roll
with Carrot, Daikon Radish,
and Snow Peas in a
Thai-inspired Spicy Sweet Sauce

This recipe takes its inspiration from the popular Thai spring roll.
The sweetness of the vegetables complements the taste of the lobster, and the spicy
sauce provides a little kick. Guests enjoy putting down their forks and knives
and eating this course with their fingers. Fry only as many rolls as you need for your
appetizer course. One roll per person is usually sufficient for a light appetizer.
You can refrigerate the remaining rolls on a plate, covered with a towel,
to cook the next day. Look for spring roll wrappers in the refrigerated section
of large supermarkets or Asian grocery stores.

Makes 8

1 teaspoon toasted sesame oil

2 large carrots, peeled and julienned

1 medium daikon radish, peeled and julienned

10 snow peas, julienned

1 (1-inch) piece of ginger, peeled and
finely chopped

1 teaspoon oyster sauce

1 tablespoon soy sauce

1 pound cooked lobster meat, chopped

8 spring roll wrappers

1 egg yolk, beaten

Vegetable oil, for frying

Cilantro Oil (see page 62)

Thai-Inspired Spicy Sweet Sauce (see page 62)

In a large sauté pan, heat the sesame oil over medium high heat. Add the carrots, daikon radish, and snow peas and stir-fry for 1 minute. Add the ginger, oyster sauce, and soy sauce and stir to combine. Remove the vegetables from the heat.

In a large bowl, combine half of the vegetable mixture with the lobster meat. Divide the mixture into eight equal portions, squeezing out any extra moisture.

On a dry work surface, lay out one spring roll wrapper. Using your hands, roll one of the portions of vegetable-and-lobster mixture into a cylinder and place in the center of the top edge of the wrapper.

Brush the egg yolk down the left and right edges of the wrapper and fold the edges over to cover the ends of the filling. Roll the filling down the length of the wrapper, tucking in the outside edges to make a tight roll. Seal the seam with more egg yolk. Repeat with the remaining wrappers and filling. The rolls can be fried immediately or kept covered with a towel in the refrigerator for up to 24 hours before frying.

Pour 2 inches of vegetable oil into a heavy skillet and heat over medium high heat until the oil reaches 350°F on a deep-fry thermometer. Carefully place the rolls in the hot oil and deep-fry for 5 minutes, or until golden brown on all sides.

Using tongs, remove the spring rolls from the oil and drain on paper towels. Slice them in half, cutting on the diagonal. Arrange the rolls on serving plates, surrounded with the remaining stir-fried vegetables. Drizzle Cilantro Oil and Thai-Inspired Spicy Sweet Sauce over the rolls.

Cilantro Oil

Makes 1 cup

1 bunch fresh cilantro

1 cup vegetable oil

Fill a medium saucepan with water and bring it to a boil. Drop the cilantro into the boiling water for a few seconds, then drain and refresh in a large bowl of ice water until cool.

Squeeze all excess liquid from the blanched cilantro and place it in the jar of a blender with the oil. Blend on high for 30 seconds, until the cilantro is puréed. Strain the oil through a fine sieve lined with cheesecloth. Store any remaining cilantro oil in a covered container in the refrigerator.

Thai-Inspired Spicy Sweet Sauce

*This recipe yields more sauce than you will need for
the Lobster Spring Roll. The remaining sauce will keep, covered, in the refrigerator
for up to two weeks. It makes a delicious stir-fry sauce for vegetables
or a flavorful dipping sauce for cooked shrimp, fried shrimp crackers, or crudités.*

Makes 2 cups

2 cups sugar

¼ cup soy sauce

¼ teaspoon hot pepper flakes (or half a dried hot pepper)

1 garlic clove, minced

In a large saucepan with a heavy bottom, combine 2 cups water with the sugar, soy sauce, hot pepper flakes, and garlic. Bring to a boil over high heat.

Reduce the heat to medium high and cook until the sauce is reduced slightly and coats the back of a spoon. Remove the dried hot pepper half, if used.

KALAMANSI
SOUR LEMON SORBET

*Now that many people have their own ice cream makers, home chefs
have discovered how easy it is to make fruit sorbets.
There's no reason to save sorbet for dessert. At the White Barn Inn,
we serve tart fruit sorbet as an intermezzo during a formal dinner. The flavor
clears the tastes of the previous course and lingers just a few minutes
on the tongue, priming the palate for the main course. This sorbet is made
from puréed kalamansi, a small, sour, limelike citrus common in the Philippines
that tastes like a cross between a lemon and a mandarin orange.
If you can't find kalamansi purée in a local gourmet store or catalog, then
substitute a mixture of pulpy lime and mandarin orange juice.*

Makes 2 quarts

2 cups sugar

4 cups kalamansi purée
(or 3 cups lime juice and 1 cup mandarin orange juice)

In a medium saucepan, combine the sugar with 3 cups of water and bring to a
boil over medium high heat. Place the kalamansi purée in a large, nonreactive
glass or stainless steel bowl and pour in the hot syrup, stirring to blend thoroughly. Alternatively, stir the lime and orange juices into the hot syrup, mixing
well. Refrigerate until cool.

Freeze in an ice cream machine, following the manufacturer's instructions.

GRILLED TOURNEDOS OF LOCAL COD LOIN
WITH CRISPY SHRIMP AND CALAMARI ON A SPRING PEA
PURÉE WITH A PIQUANT SAUCE

*This recipe plays with the English idea of fish and chips in a very refined way.
The spring pea purée is reminiscent of the mushy peas commonly eaten
in England as an accompaniment to fried fish. The crispy shrimp and potatoes offer
that deep-fried crunch, and the piquant sauce adds a refreshing, spicy contrast.
To keep the potato sticks from falling apart when frying, it is important
to coat them thoroughly with the bread crumbs.*

Serves 4

¾ pound cod loin,
cut into four tournedos (1-inch-thick slices)

6 tablespoons olive oil,
plus extra for rubbing the tournedos

Salt, freshly ground black pepper,
and cayenne to taste

½ pound fresh spring peas (1 cup shelled peas)

¼ pound cleaned calamari,
cut into bite-size rings, with tentacles

1 teaspoon fresh lemon juice

1 large potato, peeled and diced

3 tablespoons unsalted butter

2 eggs

2 tablespoons flour

⅓ cup plain bread crumbs

¾ pound Maine shrimp or rock shrimp, peeled

Vegetable oil, for deep frying

Piquant Sauce (see page 67)

Preheat a gas or charcoal grill.

Using butcher's twine, tie each cod tournedo around the perimeter to keep its shape. Rub the tournedos with a little olive oil and season with salt and pepper. Grill for 1 or 2 minutes on each side. They will be partially cooked. Remove from the grill to a plate.

Fill a medium saucepan with water and bring to a boil. Drop the peas into the boiling water and cook until tender but still bright green, about 4 minutes. Drain and refresh in a large bowl of ice water until cool, then drain again. Purée the cooked peas in a food processor, then pass the mixture through a medium sieve to remove any lumps.

Heat the 6 tablespoons of olive oil in a medium skillet over high heat. Add the calamari pieces and sear for 3 minutes, tossing occasionally. Do not overcook. Remove from the heat immediately, sprinkle with the lemon juice, and season with salt and pepper.

Preheat the oven to 350°F.

Fill a medium saucepan with water and bring to a boil over high heat. Add the diced potatoes and boil until they are easily pierced by a fork. Drain the potatoes and dry them on a baking sheet in the hot oven for 3 to 4 minutes. In a large bowl, combine the potatoes with 2 tablespoons of the butter and mash until the lumps disappear. Season with salt and pepper.

Fill a pastry bag with the potato purée. Using a quarter-inch plain tip, pipe the purée onto a sheet of waxed paper into strips 2 inches long.

In a shallow bowl, beat the eggs. Fill another shallow bowl with the flour and a third with the bread crumbs.

Season the potato sticks and shrimp to taste with salt, pepper, and cayenne. Carefully dip the potato sticks in the flour, then the beaten eggs, then the bread crumbs. Take care that the potato sticks are completely coated in the bread crumbs.

Pour 2 inches of vegetable oil into a heavy pot and heat over medium high heat until the oil reaches 350°F on a deep-fry thermometer. Carefully place the potato sticks in the hot oil and deep-fry for 4 minutes, or until golden brown. Remove the cooked sticks from the oil with a skimmer or slotted spoon and drain on paper towels. Bread and fry the shrimp in the same manner.

Place the grilled cod tournedos in a nonreactive baking dish and bake for 5 minutes, or until cooked through. While the fish is baking, reheat the pea purée in a medium saucepan with the remaining tablespoon of butter. Season to taste with salt and pepper.

To serve, spoon the pea purée in a ring in the center of each plate. Place a cod tournedo in the center of each ring and arrange the potatoes, shrimp, and calamari in a pile on one side. Drizzle with Piquant Sauce.

PIQUANT SAUCE

Makes 1 cup

4 tablespoons (½ stick) unsalted butter

¼ cup diced yellow onion

¼ cup dry, fruity white wine, such as sauvignon blanc

¼ cup champagne vinegar

8 crushed black peppercorns

2 cups Veal Jus (see page 68)

1 tablespoon Dijon mustard

Salt and freshly ground pepper

In a medium saucepan with a heavy bottom, melt the butter over medium heat. Add the onion and sauté for about 5 minutes, until translucent but not browned. Stir in the wine, vinegar, and crushed peppercorns. Cook over medium heat for 5 minutes, or until reduced by half.

Add the Veal Jus, increase the heat to medium high, and bring the mixture to a boil. Reduce over high heat until the sauce becomes thick enough to coat the back of a spoon.

Remove the pan from the heat, whisk in the mustard until it is completely incorporated, and season to taste with salt and pepper. Strain through a fine sieve.

Veal or Lamb Jus

In French kitchens, reduced meat stock, called jus, forms the base for many sauces. Use this formula to prepare lamb jus for the recipe on page 37 by substituting lamb bones for the veal bones. If you are serious about cooking, it's a good idea to keep a supply of different meat stocks and jus on hand. Whenever you are at the butcher shop, buy extra bones and roast them. Then simmer them on the stove with aromatic vegetables and herbs. When the stock has cooked for several hours, cool it to room temperature, then freeze it.

Makes 6 cups.

10 pounds veal or lamb bones

½ pound (about 1 cup) diced mixed aromatic vegetables,
such as carrot, leek, onion, and celery

1 cup dry red wine

4 medium tomatoes, diced

1 garlic clove, crushed

2 dozen fresh herb stems, such as thyme, rosemary, and tarragon

Preheat the oven to 450°F.

Place the bones in one or more large roasting pans and roast for about 30 minutes, turning occasionally, until golden brown. Add the diced vegetables and continue to roast for 5 minutes more.

Transfer the roasted bones and vegetables to a large stockpot. Add the wine and enough water to cover the bones. Bring to a boil over high heat. Skim off and discard any scum that rises to the surface.

Add the tomatoes, garlic, and herb stems to the stock. Reduce the heat to low and simmer for 4 to 6 hours, until the stock becomes dark and rich. Strain the stock through a colander, discarding the solids, and pour it into a clean saucepan. Cook over medium heat for about 40 minutes, until reduced by half.

Fill the kitchen sink half-full with ice and cold water. Cool the jus by placing the saucepan in the ice bath until cooled to room temperature. The jus will keep in the refrigerator for a couple of days, or in an airtight container in the freezer for up to two months.

"Twice-Baked" Rhubarb Crêpe Soufflé with Buttermilk Ice Cream

Although it sounds complicated, most of this dish can be prepared three hours ahead of time. It combines the texture of a crêpe with the fluffiness of a soufflé and tempers the tartness of rhubarb with sugar and apple liqueur.

Serves 4

CRÊPES

2 eggs

3 tablespoons sugar

½ cup half and half cream

2 tablespoons toasted almond flour or finely ground toasted almonds

2 tablespoons flour

2 tablespoons unsalted butter, melted

In a large bowl, beat the eggs until foamy. Add the sugar and beat until combined. Add the cream, almond flour, flour, and melted butter, beating continuously to form a smooth batter.

Heat a 6-inch nonstick skillet over medium heat. Ladle about 3 tablespoons of the crêpe mixture into the skillet and swirl to cover the bottom of the pan. Cook over medium heat until the edges begin to turn light brown. Carefully flip the crêpe and continue cooking for 30 seconds. Transfer the crêpe to a plate and repeat until all the batter has been used.

SOUFFLÉ

1 cup milk

3 tablespoons unsalted butter

3 tablespoons flour

¾ ounce Calvados

3 tablespoons granulated sugar, plus additional, for dusting

½ cup Rhubarb Purée (see page 49)

4 eggs, separated

Confectioners' sugar

Buttermilk Ice Cream (see page 72)

In a small saucepan with a heavy bottom, bring the milk to a boil. Remove from the heat and keep warm.

In a medium saucepan, melt the butter over medium low heat and whisk in the flour. Gradually pour in the hot milk to form a smooth sauce, whisking constantly to remove any lumps.

Remove from the heat and stir in the Calvados, sugar, and Rhubarb Purée. Beat the egg yolks and whisk them into the mixture, continuing to whisk until the soufflé base returns to room temperature.

Preheat the oven to 350°F.

In a large bowl, whisk the egg whites until they form stiff peaks. Carefully fold the beaten egg whites into the soufflé base.

Butter four ramekins (3½ inches in diameter, 1½ inches deep) and coat them with granulated sugar, shaking out any excess. Line each ramekin with one crêpe, tucking it carefully into the sides and bottom. Pour the soufflé mixture into the prepared ramekins. Place the ramekins in a baking pan and pour boiling water into the pan to reach almost halfway up the sides of the ramekins. Carefully place the pan in the oven and bake for 30 minutes, until the soufflés are golden on top and puffed.

Remove the pan from the oven. Remove the soufflés from the water bath and allow them to cool. They can be prepared 3 hours ahead of time up to this point.

Before serving, preheat the oven to 425°F.

Place the soufflés on a baking dish and bake for 5 minutes. The soufflés will collapse. Remove the soufflés from the oven and turn them out, crêpe side up, onto dessert plates. Sprinkle with confectioners' sugar and serve hot, with Buttermilk Ice Cream.

Buttermilk Ice Cream

Buttermilk has such a rich, tangy flavor.
When made into ice cream,
it tastes a little like Devonshire clotted cream.

Makes about 1½ quarts

2 cups heavy cream

2 cups buttermilk

1 vanilla bean

1 cup sugar

12 egg yolks

In a large saucepan with a heavy bottom, combine the heavy cream and buttermilk. Split the vanilla bean and scrape the seeds into the pan, then add the bean. Add ½ cup of the sugar and bring to a boil over medium high heat, stirring regularly to make sure that the mixture does not scorch on the bottom of the pan. Remove from the heat and let cool for a few minutes.

In a large bowl, beat the egg yolks. Add the remaining sugar and stir just to combine. Pour a small amount of the warm cream mixture into the egg yolks, stirring to temper and warm the egg yolks slightly. Then gradually pour the egg mixture into the saucepan with the cream mixture, stirring until thoroughly blended. Cook over medium heat, stirring constantly, until thick enough to coat the back of a wooden spoon.

Strain the custard through a fine sieve and allow it to cool completely. Freeze in an ice cream machine, following the manufacturer's instructions.

Breakfast by the Pool

BREAKFAST FRUIT BOWL

*By cutting several different kinds of fruit into half-inch dice and
tossing them together, you can create a confetti-like salad that accentuates
the fresh colors and textures of seasonal produce.*

Serves 8

1 cup sugar

1 cinnamon stick

1 vanilla bean

1 cantaloupe

1 honeydew melon

1 pineapple

4 oranges

2 kiwis

1 cup raspberries

In a medium saucepan, combine the sugar and cinnamon stick with 2 cups of water. Split the vanilla bean, scraping the seeds into the pan, and add the bean. Bring to a boil over medium high heat, stirring to dissolve the sugar. Remove the syrup from the heat. When it is cool, strain and discard the vanilla bean and cinnamon stick.

Remove the rind and seeds from the melons and cut into $\frac{1}{2}$-inch dice. Remove the skin and core from the pineapple and cut the fruit into $\frac{1}{2}$-inch dice. Peel the oranges, divide the fruit into sections, and cut each section in half. Peel and slice the kiwis. Rinse and drain the raspberries.

In a large bowl, gently combine the fruits with the syrup. The fruit salad will keep in the refrigerator, covered, for 2 hours before serving.

POACHED EGGS ON
KENNEBUNKPORT LOBSTER HASH

*This dish is inspired by the quintessential New England dish, hash.
Lobster is considered the queen of seafood, so it may seem a bit decadent to make
hash out of it—but a bit of decadence is what guests have come
to expect from the White Barn Inn. This version combines bits of lobster
with potato, bound with a sauce made from lobster bisque. If you prepare the
lobster bisque a day ahead of time, this recipe makes a quickly assembled brunch
dish sure to surprise and impress your guests. The eggs can be poached
2 to 3 hours ahead of time and kept in chilled water, to be reheated just before
serving. Any remaining lobster bisque can be enjoyed later for dinner.*

Serves 4

1 teaspoon white vinegar

Salt and freshly ground pepper

4 eggs

1 tablespoon olive oil

2 cups peeled and diced potato

2 tablespoons unsalted butter

1 cup diced, cooked lobster meat

4 cooked lobster claws, shelled, with meat in one piece

1 cup Lobster Bisque (see page 77)

1 tablespoon chopped mixed fresh herbs,
such as chives, tarragon, and parsley

4 long fresh chives, for garnish

Fill a shallow pan with water and add the white vinegar and a pinch of salt. Bring to a simmer over medium heat. Gently break the eggs into the simmering water. Cook over medium heat for 3 to 4 minutes, until soft-poached. Using a slotted spoon, remove the eggs to a pan filled with ice water and reserve until ready to reheat just before serving. Reserve the poaching liquid.

Heat the olive oil in a large sauté pan over medium high heat. Add the potatoes and cook, turning frequently, for about 8 minutes, until golden brown.

Add the butter to the pan and reduce the heat to medium. Gently stir in the lobster meat, lobster claws, and Lobster Bisque, and cook for 3 to 4 minutes. Add the fresh herbs and season to taste with salt and pepper.

Reheat the eggs in the poaching liquid for 2 to 3 minutes. While the eggs are reheating, remove the claws from the pan and divide the hash among four serving plates. Top each serving with a poached egg and garnish with a lobster claw and a chive.

THICK TOWELS, NUBBY LOOFAHS,
AND AN ARRAY OF LIGHTLY SCENTED BODY PRODUCTS
ENHANCE THE PLEASURE OF BATHING AT
THE WHITE BARN INN, WHERE ALL SUITES INCLUDE
SPACIOUS BATHROOMS WITH DEEP
WHIRLPOOL TUBS.

Lobster Bisque

Makes 2 quarts

4 tablespoons (½ stick) unsalted butter

1 medium onion, diced

1 garlic clove

6 medium tomatoes, diced

1 sprig fresh thyme

1 sprig fresh parsley

1 sprig fresh tarragon

½ cup white dessert wine, such as muscat

1 cup brandy

4 cups heavy cream

4 cups Lobster Stock (see page 78)

1 teaspoon lobster roe, if available

Salt, freshly ground pepper, and cayenne

Juice of ½ lemon

In a large saucepan with a heavy bottom, melt the butter over medium heat. Add the onion, garlic, tomatoes, and herbs and sauté for about 5 minutes, until the onions are translucent but not browned.

Add the wine and brandy and increase the heat to medium high, cooking the mixture until it is reduced by half. Add the cream and lobster stock and bring to a boil. Reduce the heat to medium and cook for about 15 minutes, whisking occasionally, until thick enough to coat the back of a spoon.

Whisk in the lobster roe, if available, and bring the soup back to a boil. Strain the soup through a fine sieve into a clean saucepan and season to taste with salt, pepper, cayenne, and lemon juice before serving.

LOBSTER STOCK

You will need 6½ pounds of lobster to yield 5 pounds of lobster shells.
The Lobster Hash recipe calls for just 1 cup of lobster meat, so if
you make this stock a day in advance, you can enjoy a dinner of boiled lobster
as a dividend. In a restaurant kitchen, nothing is wasted—hence the addition
of fresh herb stems to this flavorful stock.

Makes 1 quart

5 pounds lobster shells, head cavity cleaned

1 pound (about 1 cup) diced mixed aromatic vegetables,
such as carrot, leek, onion, and celery

10 medium ripe tomatoes, chopped

2 cups dry white wine, such as chardonnay

1 cup V-8 juice

1 dozen mixed fresh herb stems,
such as thyme, parsley, tarragon, and dill

1 garlic clove

Preheat the oven to 450°F.

In a roasting pan, combine the lobster shells, vegetables, and tomatoes and roast for 15 minutes, stirring occasionally, until the shells have a dry, cooked appearance and the vegetables are lightly browned.

Transfer the roasted shells and vegetables to a large stockpot. Add the wine, V-8 juice, and enough water to cover all the ingredients. Bring the stock to a boil over high heat, skimming off any scum that rises to the surface.

Reduce the heat to a simmer and add the herbs and garlic. Simmer the stock for at least 3 hours, until it turns a deep reddish-brown and has a rich flavor and aroma.

Strain the stock into a clean pot and cook over high heat until reduced by half. The stock will keep in the refrigerator for a few days, or up to two months in an airtight container in the freezer.

PoppySeed Muffins

*In this recipe, the pastry flour is sifted twice
to ensure a light, moist muffin.*

Makes 16 small or 8 regular muffins

2 cups pastry flour, sifted twice

$\frac{1}{4}$ teaspoon salt

$\frac{1}{2}$ cup sugar

1 teaspoon baking powder

4 tablespoons poppyseeds

$3\frac{1}{2}$ tablespoons unsalted butter, melted

$\frac{1}{2}$ cup sour cream

2 eggs

1 drop maple extract

Preheat the oven to 400°F. Butter a muffin tin. In a large bowl, sift together the flour, salt, sugar, baking powder, and poppyseeds.

In a medium bowl, combine the melted butter, sour cream, and eggs and beat for 7 minutes. Add the egg mixture to the dry ingredients and beat with an electric mixer on low speed until thoroughly combined. Add the maple extract and beat until combined. Spoon the batter into the buttered muffin cups, filling them to the top. Bake for about 10 minutes, until the muffins have risen and are light gold on top.

CHOCOLATE CHIP
MUFFINS

Makes 16 small or 8 regular muffins

10 tablespoons (1¼ sticks) unsalted butter,
at room temperature

2 cups sugar

½ cup milk, at room temperature

2¼ cups all-purpose flour

¼ cup unsweetened cocoa powder

¼ teaspoon salt

1 tablespoon baking powder

4 large eggs

1 cup chocolate chips

Preheat the oven to 400°F. Butter a muffin tin. In a large bowl, cream the butter with the sugar. Gradually add the milk and mix until thoroughly combined.

In a large bowl, sift together the flour, cocoa powder, salt, and baking powder.

Using an electric mixer on low speed, gradually add half the beaten eggs to the butter mixture. Add half of the dry ingredients and mix until thoroughly incorporated. Repeat with the remaining beaten eggs and dry ingredients. Add the chocolate chips and mix on medium speed for 7 minutes to aerate the muffins.

Spoon the batter into the buttered muffin cups, filling them to the top. Bake for about 10 minutes, until the muffins have risen and are light gold on top.

Spring Ingredients

FOREST MUSHROOMS

These little mushrooms grow on the forest floor in the spring and early summer. They have a wonderful, woodsy taste—slightly nutty, with a peppery finish. Serve them very lightly sautéed to capture their delicate flavor. Chanterelles, or yellow-foot mushrooms, known as girolles in France, are raised domestically year-round on the East Coast.

FIDDLEHEAD FERNS

In spring the forest floor is covered with baby ferns shaped like the head of a fiddle. Fiddlehead ferns have a unique flavor that combines the fresh green taste of asparagus with the richer notes of artichoke. Unless you are an experienced forager, it's best to buy packaged fiddlehead ferns in spring rather than forage for them, as not all forest ferns are edible.

ASPARAGUS

The first asparagus of spring are delicate and delicious. The tender tops, lightly steamed, are a wonderful addition to a cold salad of cooked vegetables. They also make a beautiful bed of color beneath grilled fish.

WATERCRESS

Watercress has a robust, peppery flavor with a touch of bitterness. Served raw and dressed with a champagne vinaigrette, it makes a delicious salad with steamed beets. When cooked, watercress assumes a soft, velvety texture and makes a wonderful base for a cream soup.

SPINACH

Spinach is a very versatile ingredient—fresh-tasting, like watercress, but milder in flavor. Baby spinach leaves form the basis for a great spring salad. Creamed spinach is a delightful spring comfort food that celebrates the bright color and tender texture of this leafy green.

RHUBARB

Rhubarb is considered by many to be a rather plain vegetable, but it has a beautiful color and versatile flavor that adds tartness to both sweet and savory recipes.

CHIVES

Chives are one of the first herbs to grow in spring. Their mild, oniony flavor and fresh green color provide great accents in soups, salads, and sauces. Their long, slender shape makes chives an ideal garnish.

Summer at the
WHITE BARN INN

Summer is short in Maine—which is all the more reason to surrender completely to its pleasures. One of the best places to surrender is on a boat, skimming along the water with a light wind cooling your skin. From the vantage point of the sea, the Maine shore reveals its varied nature, with rocky promontories where waves toss veils of foam into the sky, protected coves where surf laps against sandy beaches, and bright green lawns that spill down to the sea from rambling Shingle Style cottages.

Hot summer days call for light lunches that can be easily prepared and eaten on the go. Maine's famous lobster roll—tender morsels of lobster meat tossed with a lemony mayonnaise and spooned into a roll—is a perfect expression of summer's simpler fare. When guests require a picnic lunch, White Barn Inn chef Jonathan Cartwright transforms this ubiquitous sandwich into something special by serving it on a roll with a sturdy texture that stands up better to the moist filling than the commercial rolls typically used.

Deep-sea fishermen look forward to the summer months with eager anticipation, dreaming of pulling in one of the giant bluefin tuna that ply the waters, or landing a striped bass, a magnificent fighting fish that leaps through the surf. Scallops, mussels, and clams are easily gathered, and lobsters fill the lobstermen's traps. A formal dinner at the White Barn Inn offers an opportunity to taste the bounty of summer's sea without having to go to the trouble of catching it. On summer menus the chef pairs each fish with sauces ranging from the delicate to the spicy, as well as such locally grown produce as heirloom tomatoes, bright red peppers, and tender peas.

Next to boats, porches offer summer's best perches. Nearly all the houses along Maine's coast boast porches where grills stand in as outdoor stoves, picnic tables serve as second dining rooms, and comfortable wicker rocking chairs invite long spells of sitting, reading, or chatting with friends. On the Fourth of July, year-round and seasonal residents gather on porches and lawns for elaborate picnics made easy by the sharing of cooking and cleaning tasks. Thanks to its hard shell and firm flesh, lobster stands up well to the grill. While planning crops of tomatoes, squash, beans, and corn. Fruit farmers open their fields to amateur pickers, who delight in gathering their own strawberries and eating them straight from the plant. Cold fruit soups—served year-round at the White Barn Inn as intermezzos between heavier courses—take on a special appeal in summer when so much sun-sweetened fruit is available. A chilled soup of strawberries puréed with mandarin orange juice and champagne or watermelon blended with the juice of Bing cherries perfectly captures the

Fruit farmers open their fields to amateur pickers, who delight in gathering their own strawberries and eating them straight from the plant.

a menu for a Fourth of July cookout, chef Cartwright created a mayonnaise infused with smoked tomato to complement the flavor of grilled lobster. Served with a trio of salads featuring baby lettuces, sweet corn, and wild rice, and followed with strawberry shortcake, this entrée celebrates the robust colors, textures, and flavors of the season.

Each summer, stands spring up along the country roads where local farmers sell a selection of freshly harvested produce that changes weekly as their fields yield essence of summer. For hot summer afternoons, the chef also recommends iced fruit teas flavored with peaches, raspberries, or whatever fruit is at hand.

The following menus and recipes suggest just a few ways of celebrating New England's summer harvest. Mix and match them to create meals that involve as much or little effort as you want to expend. No matter where you live, summer always delivers plentiful, colorful, flavorful produce that is a pleasure to cook and to eat. Enjoy it while it lasts.

SUMMER MENUS

Fourth of July Party

Edible Martinis

Iced Watermelon and Bing Cherry Soup

Grilled Maine Lobster with Barbecue Mayonnaise,
Wild Rice Salad, and Grilled Corn Salad

Local Summer Greens with
Carrot Vinaigrette

Strawberry Shortcake

·

A Simple Boating Lunch

Maine Lobster Roll

Carrot Hummus Roll-ups

Peach Iced Tea

Miniature Berry Muffins

A Summer Tea Party

Raspberry Iced Tea

Homemade Lemonade

Tomato and Cheddar Sandwiches

Cold-Smoked Salmon Sandwiches

Egg Salad Sandwiches

Scones with Strawberry Jam

Warm Blueberry Petit Fours

•

A Summer Seafood Dinner

Tandoori-Crusted Soft-Shell Crab with Avocado and Lime Salsa

Grilled Yellowfin Tuna Loin on Summer Corn and Shellfish Hash
with Smoked Tomato Coulis

Strawberry, Mandarin Orange, and Champagne Soup

Pan-Roasted Striped Bass and Lobster Ravioli with
Summer Zucchini Ribbons and Saffron Foam

A Selection of Summer Sorbets

•

A Summer Cocktail

Watermelon Cosmopolitan

Fourth of July Party

This menu offers a wonderful way to celebrate Independence Day, or any summer day when you feel like lighting the grill and inviting friends over for a special meal. If you prepare the Cold-Smoked Salmon and Barbecue Mayonnaise in advance, you can finish cooking this meal in an hour or two. Or divide the recipes among your friends and host a casual summer potluck party.

EDIBLE MARTINIS

This dish is part cocktail, part canapé. Eat the salmon first,
then drink the dill-infused vodka while it's still icy cold. Save the remaining
smoked salmon to make tea sandwiches (see pages 116–117) or serve it
with poached eggs for a special breakfast.

Serves 4

½ cup Dill-Infused Vodka (see page 92)

8 slices Cold-Smoked Salmon (see page 91)

4 lemon twists

8 Sicilian jumbo green olives

Chilled cooked crab claws, for garnish (optional)

Ice four large martini glasses. In a cocktail shaker, combine the Dill-Infused Vodka with ice and shake to chill.

Curl two slices of salmon in the bottom of each martini glass. Spear two olives and a lemon twist on each of four cocktail picks and place one in each glass with the salmon.

Pour 1 ounce (⅛ cup) iced vodka into each glass over the salmon. Garnish with a chilled, cooked crab claw.

COLD-SMOKED SALMON

*This simple, flavorful salmon can be stored in an airtight container
in the refrigerator for up to ten days after it's been smoked.*

Makes 2 pounds

1½ cups kosher salt

2 cups sugar

2 pounds salmon filet, in one piece

2 pounds wood chips, for smoking (hickory, maple, or apple)

In a large bowl, combine the salt and sugar. Press the salmon filet into the mixture, coating it evenly. Place the seasoned salmon on a large plate or in a nonreactive glass or stainless steel baking dish and cover it with plastic wrap. Place the salmon in the refrigerator to cure for 24 hours.

Rinse the salt and sugar off the salmon under cold water. To cold-smoke the salmon using an outdoor charcoal grill, place half the wood chips in the bottom of the grill and light them. Place the salmon skin-side down on the grill grate and cover the grill, leaving a small gap or adjusting the chimney to a slightly open position. Check from time to time to make sure that the chips are smoking and that the salmon is not getting so hot that it is cooking. (If this happens, the flesh will start to turn a lighter shade.) If the salmon is cooking, place a metal tray filled with ice between the salmon and the wood chips and continue smoking. Add more chips and relight as necessary to smoke the salmon for a total of 2½ hours.

Let the smoked salmon cool, then cover with plastic wrap. Refrigerate for at least 12 hours. To serve, remove the rib and pin bones with your fingers or tweezers. Slice the salmon thinly using a very sharp knife.

DILL-INFUSED VODKA

*Any remaining flavored vodka will keep in the refrigerator
for several weeks and makes a wonderful addition to Bloody Marys.*

Makes 32 ounces

1 bunch fresh dill

10 wide strips lemon zest

1 (32-ounce) bottle lemon-flavored vodka

Wash the dill and combine with the lemon zest in a large jar or pitcher. Add the vodka. Cover and leave to infuse in the refrigerator for 24 hours. Strain the vodka, discarding the dill and lemon zest, and store in the freezer or refrigerator for up to two months.

ICED WATERMELON AND BING CHERRY SOUP

*The trick to making chilled fruit soups is to keep them light and well balanced in flavor.
A soup that's too sweet will overwhelm the palate. The addition of champagne adds an
effervescent note. Be sure to serve this as soon as you stir in the chilled champagne.*

Serves 4

2 pounds watermelon, peeled, seeded, and cut into chunks

1 pound Bing cherries, pitted

1 cup white dessert wine, such as muscat

1 cup chilled champagne

In a food processor, purée the watermelon, cherries, and white wine until smooth. Strain through a fine sieve into a serving bowl or pitcher, cover, and refrigerate. Just before serving, stir in the chilled champagne.

Grilled Maine Lobster with Barbecue Mayonnaise, Wild Rice Salad, and Grilled Corn Salad

It's important to relax and socialize with your guests when hosting a barbecue. Because the lobsters are steamed before being grilled, you can prepare them partially in advance. The grilling takes only 10 minutes, which permits the hosts plenty of time to relax.

Serves 4

2 (1½ pound) Maine lobsters

1 cup Barbecue Mayonnaise (see page 96)

Local Summer Greens with Carrot Vinaigrette (see page 97)

Grilled Corn Salad (see page 100)

Wild Rice Salad (see page 101)

Bring a large stockpot filled with water to a boil and plunge the live lobsters head-first into the pot, cooking them for 5 minutes in the rapidly boiling water. Remove from the water and drain.

Using a large, heavy chef's knife, split the cooked lobsters in half lengthwise. Clean out the head cavities, discarding the contents. With the knife, make long slits in the shells of the claws and knuckles (but do not remove the shells.) The cooled, steamed lobsters can be kept covered with plastic wrap in the refrigerator for up 24 hours before grilling.

Preheat a charcoal grill to high. Place the partially steamed lobsters flesh-side down on the oiled grate of the grill and cook directly over the coals for 5 minutes.

Turn the lobsters, placing them shell side down on the grill grate. Brush the exposed lobster meat liberally with Barbecue Mayonnaise and cook directly over the coals for 5 minutes.

To serve, place the grilled lobster halves on a bed of Local Summer Greens with Carrot Vinaigrette. Fill the head cavity with Grilled Corn Salad and place a mound of Wild Rice Salad next to the lobster.

BARBECUE MAYONNAISE

Any remaining Barbecue Mayonnaise can be kept in the refrigerator for a week and makes a wonderful substitute for regular mayonnaise in lobster rolls or other sandwiches.

Makes 2 cups

Wood chips, for smoking (hickory, maple, or apple)

6 ripe tomatoes

1 cup plus 1 tablespoon olive oil

1 garlic clove, minced

¼ cup chopped shallots

1 teaspoon prepared horseradish

2 egg yolks

1 teaspoon Dijon mustard

¼ cup red wine vinegar

2 drops Tabasco sauce

2 drops Worcestershire sauce

1 teaspoon fresh lemon juice, or to taste

Salt and freshly ground pepper

Light two handfuls of wood chips in the bottom of a charcoal grill. Cut the tomatoes in half and place them skin-side down on the grill grate over the wood chips. Cover the grill, leaving a small gap or adjusting the chimney to a slightly open position, and smoke the tomatoes for 20 minutes.

In a medium sauté pan, heat 1 tablespoon of olive oil over medium heat. Add the garlic and shallots and cook until transparent but not brown.

In the jar of a blender or food processor, combine the cooled, smoked tomatoes, the cooked garlic and shallots, and the horseradish and purée until smooth. With the motor running, add the egg yolks, mustard, vinegar, and Tabasco.

With the motor still running, gradually add the remaining olive oil, Worcestershire sauce, and lemon juice.

Season to taste with salt, pepper, and lemon juice. This mayonnaise can be stored in an airtight container in the refrigerator for one week.

LOCAL SUMMER GREENS
WITH CARROT VINAIGRETTE

When serving tender baby lettuce, it is important
not to overdress the salad. Use just a bit of dressing, toss, and taste.
If all the greens are lightly coated with dressing, then serve
the salad at once. If the greens seem dry, add a little more dressing and
toss lightly. Make sure that the pansies and nasturtiums
are free of any garden pesticides or sprays.

Serves 4

3 heads baby Lola Rossa lettuce

3 heads baby red Bibb lettuce

3 heads baby green Bibb lettuce

1 small bunch arugula

2 small heads curly endive

3 pansies

20 baby asparagus

1 golden beet

1 cup Carrot Vinaigrette (see page 98)

4 nasturtium flowers

20 cherry tomatoes

Small bunch chives, finely chopped

1 small carrot, grated

Wash and dry all the greens. Remove the petals from the pansies and reserve.

Bring a medium skillet of water to a boil over medium high heat and add the asparagus. Blanch until tender, 2 to 3 minutes. Refresh in cold water and drain well.

Preheat the oven to 400°F.

Wrap the beet in aluminum foil and place it in a roasting pan in the center of the oven. Roast for about 30 minutes, or until tender. Allow it to cool, then peel and slice thinly.

In a large salad bowl, toss the greens with the Carrot Vinaigrette.

To serve, divide the dressed greens among four serving plates. Surround with the asparagus, beet slices, and tomatoes, drizzling with additional dressing. Garnish the salad with pansy petals, whole nasturtiums, chives, and grated carrot.

CARROT VINAIGRETTE

Fresh juice infuses this light vinaigrette with the sweet taste of spring's first carrots. If you don't have an appliance to make your own carrot juice, buy freshly made carrot juice. Don't use prebottled juice, as it will not have the sweet, fresh flavor required for this vinaigrette.

Makes about 2 cups

3 medium carrots, juiced (½ cup
fresh carrot juice)

½ teaspoon Dijon mustard

1 cup extra-virgin olive oil

½ cup white wine vinegar

Salt and freshly ground pepper

Pour the carrot juice into a medium bowl and whisk in the mustard. Gradually add the olive oil, continuing to whisk until the mixture is emulsified.

Whisk in the vinegar and add salt and pepper to taste. This dressing will keep in the refrigerator, tightly covered, for three days.

Grilled Corn Salad

*This salad is a perfect way to showcase
the sweet flavor of summer corn.*

Serves 4

4 ears fresh corn, husks on

1 red onion, diced

2 ripe medium tomatoes, diced

1 teaspoon chopped fresh parsley

1 tablespoon rice wine vinegar

¼ cup olive oil

Salt and freshly ground pepper

Preheat a charcoal grill.

Without removing the husks, place the ears of corn on the grate of the hot grill
and cook for 10 minutes, turning occasionally. The husks will turn black. Remove
the corn from the grill and allow to cool. Remove the husks and silks and cut the
kernels off the cob into a large bowl.

Add the diced red onion and tomatoes to the corn. Then add the parsley, vinegar, olive oil, salt, and pepper and toss well to combine. The salad can be prepared
up to one day in advance. Cover and refrigerate until ready to serve.

WILD RICE SALAD

Although this recipe calls for carrots, other summer vegetables
such as peppers, zucchini, tomatoes, and celery can be added. Just use
your imagination and the freshest farm produce available.

Serves 4

1½ cups raw wild rice (early harvest, if available)

1 large carrot, diced

½ medium yellow onion, diced

3 tablespoons Homemade Mayonnaise (see page 108),
or a good-quality commercial brand

1 teaspoon chopped mixed fresh herbs, such as chives, tarragon, and chervil

Salt and freshly ground pepper

In a large saucepan, bring 6 cups of salted water to a boil. Add the rice, reduce the heat to low, and cover. Cook for 15 minutes, or until the grains are just beginning to split open and you see the white inside. Drain the rice and let cool.

In a large bowl, combine the cooled rice with the carrot, onion, mayonnaise, and herbs and toss thoroughly. Season to taste with salt and pepper. Cover and refrigerate until ready to serve.

CHIVES

THE WHITE BARN INN KITCHEN STAFF MAINTAINS
AN HERB GARDEN, SO THAT SEASONAL FLAVORINGS CAN
BE USED WITHIN HOURS OF BEING HARVESTED.
CHIVES THRIVE IN THE GARDEN AND MAKE A FLAVORFUL,
ATTRACTIVE GARNISH FOR SPRING
AND SUMMER DISHES.

STRAWBERRY SHORTCAKE

*This classic dessert is one of the best ways to enjoy
perfectly ripe summer strawberries.
The crumbly shortcake biscuits absorb some of the
marinated strawberries' juices, and the vanilla-flavored
whipped cream provides a mellow contrast
to the berries' tangy flavor.*

Serves 6

6 Shortcake Biscuits (see page 104)

2 cups Marinated Strawberries (see page 105)

Vanilla-Flavored Whipped Cream (see page 105)

Place one biscuit, split in half, on each of six serving plates. Spoon equal amounts of Marinated Strawberries over each biscuit. Drizzle any remaining juice over each serving. Top with a heaping spoonful of Vanilla-Flavored Whipped Cream. Serve immediately.

SHORTCAKE BISCUITS

*In the White Barn Inn kitchen, we have a variety of flours
on hand. Some flours are made from hard wheat, which has a higher gluten
(or starch) content, and others from soft wheat. This recipe calls for
a mixture of bread and pastry flour. Four cups of all-purpose flour can be
substituted for the combination of these two flours.*

Makes 10

1½ cups bread flour

2½ cups pastry flour

½ teaspoon salt

4 tablespoons baking powder

¾ cup sugar

12 tablespoons (1½ sticks) cold
unsalted butter

3 eggs

1 teaspoon poppy seeds (optional)

1 egg yolk, beaten

2 tablespoons milk

In a large bowl, sift together the flours, salt, baking powder, and sugar. Cut in the
butter and mix until crumbs begin to form.

In a small bowl, beat the eggs. Combine the eggs gradually with the flour mixture to form a dough. Cover and allow to rest in a cool place for 10 minutes.

Preheat the oven to 350°F.

Lightly flour a dry surface and a rolling pin. Roll the dough out to a thickness
of ½ inch. Using a 3-inch cookie cutter, cut the dough into ten round biscuits. In a
small bowl, mix the egg yolk with the milk. Brush the top of each biscuit with the
egg yolk mixture. Bake for 8 minutes, until golden brown.

MARINATED STRAWBERRIES

The sugar draws the juices out of the strawberries.
If you marinate the strawberries for less than six hours, the juices
will not be completely released. Do not marinate the strawberries
for much longer, however, as the fruit will turn mushy.

Makes 2 cups

2 cups strawberries, hulled

½ cup sugar

Cut any large strawberries in half and leave the smaller ones whole. In a large bowl, sprinkle the sugar over the strawberries and toss to combine. Cover and refrigerate for 6 hours, stirring occasionally.

VANILLA-FLAVORED WHIPPED CREAM

You can prepare the whipped cream up to 3 hours ahead of serving time and keep it
in the refrigerator, covered in plastic wrap, until you are ready to serve dessert.

Makes about 3 cups

2 cups heavy cream

¼ vanilla bean, halved lengthwise

3 tablespoons confectioners' sugar

Pour the cream into a large bowl. Scrape the seeds from the vanilla bean into the cream, reserving the bean for another use.

Add the sugar and, using an electric mixer, whip until the cream forms soft peaks. Serve immediately or cover and refrigerate until ready to use.

A Simple
Boating Lunch

When planning a picnic to eat on the water, it's nice to avoid packing cutlery. This simple, delectable lunch features finger food that is easy to transport and to eat.

MAINE LOBSTER ROLL

Because the filling in this salad is moist,
wait until you're ready to eat to spoon it into the rolls.
A firm-textured roll stands up best to this filling, so it's best
to buy freshly baked rolls from a local bakery
for these sandwiches. Be sure to keep the mayonnaise-based
filling chilled until serving time.

Makes 4

1 pound (2 cups) freshly cooked lobster meat,
roughly chopped

3 tablespoons Homemade Mayonnaise (see page 108),
or a good-quality commercial brand

4 tablespoons peeled, diced cucumber

Salt and freshly ground pepper

4 firm, 6-inch-long rolls

In a large bowl, combine the lobster, mayonnaise, and cucumber. Season with salt and pepper. Cover and refrigerate for up to 4 hours, until ready to serve. Just before serving, cut the rolls lengthwise and fill with lobster salad.

HOMEMADE MAYONNAISE

*This is absolutely delicious, and so easy to make by hand.
As with all emulsion sauces, however, there are a few potential pitfalls
to watch out for. If the mayonnaise seems to become
too thick while you're adding the olive oil, just whisk in an extra
tablespoon of vinegar before adding the remaining oil.
Then add only one tablespoon of vinegar, instead of two, at the end
of the recipe. If the oil looks like it is separating from the other
ingredients, whisk in the tablespoon of hot water
during that stage instead of at the end of the preparation.
These tips should help ensure that your homemade mayonnaise
is a success. Homemade mayonnaise will keep 4 to 5 days
refrigerated in an airtight container.*

Makes 1½ cups

2 egg yolks

1 tablespoon Dijon mustard

4 tablespoons champagne vinegar

1 cup extra-virgin olive oil

Salt and freshly ground pepper

In a large mixing bowl, whisk together the egg yolks, mustard, and 2 table-spoons of the vinegar. Whisking vigorously, gradually add the oil, pouring it into the bowl in a thin stream. When all the oil is incorporated, whisk in the remaining vinegar and 1 tablespoon of hot water. Season to taste with salt and pepper. Cover and refrigerate until ready to use.

CARROT HUMMUS ROLL-UPS

*A vegetable roll-up is very satisfying—and a great way to make sure
you eat your vegetables. The addition of carrots to the hummus
gives this sandwich a vibrant color, and the grilled vegetables
stand out brightly and beautifully, too.*

Makes 4 roll-ups

1 cup peeled, sliced carrots

1 tablespoon tahini

1 garlic clove

1 zucchini, sliced ⅛ inch thick

1 eggplant, sliced ⅛ inch thick

1 yellow squash, sliced ⅛ inch thick

1 bunch asparagus, woody ends trimmed

1 red bell pepper, cored, seeded,
and cut into 2-inch squares

1 cup extra-virgin olive oil

Salt and freshly ground pepper

4 pieces lavash flatbread, each about 10 x 12 inches

2 tomatoes, sliced

2 cups mixed lettuce leaves

Bring a medium saucepan of salted water to boil. Add the sliced carrots and cook just until tender, 10 to 15 minutes. Drain and cool.

In the bowl of a food processor, combine the cooked carrots, tahini, and garlic, and purée to form a smooth spread.

Preheat a gas or charcoal grill. Toss the zucchini, eggplant, squash, asparagus, and pepper with olive oil, salt, and red pepper. Arrange them on the grill grate directly over the heat and cook until tender but not burned. Each vegetable may require a different cooking time, so watch carefully and remove as soon as it is grilled to tenderness. Remove the blackened pepper skins, if you like.

Lay the flatbread on a work surface. Spread each piece with carrot hummus. Arrange some of the grilled vegetables on top of the hummus. Top the vegetables with tomato slices and lettuce leaves and season with salt and pepper to taste. Roll each sandwich up into a tight cylinder, securing with toothpicks, if necessary.

PEACH ICED TEA

*If you're taking this tea on a picnic, pour the peach and tea infusion
into a pitcher and chill it before transferring it to an insulated thermal container.
Rub some extra lemon juice on the peach wedges to keep them from discoloring,
and store them in a separate container.*

Makes about 3 quarts

1 cup sugar

Juice of ½ lemon

4 firm, ripe peaches

4 tablespoons Darjeeling tea leaves

In a medium saucepan, combine the sugar with 1 cup of water and bring to a boil over high heat. Continue to cook over medium heat, stirring to dissolve the sugar. When the sugar is dissolved, add the lemon juice and remove from the heat.

Meanwhile, remove the pits from two peaches and roughly dice the flesh, leaving the peaches unpeeled.

In the jar of a blender, combine the sugar syrup and diced peaches and purée until smooth. Strain through a sieve and reserve in a small pitcher.

In a kettle, bring 4 cups of water to a boil. While the water is boiling, remove the pit from one peach and roughly dice the flesh. Place the tea leaves and diced peach in a heat-resistant pitcher. Add the boiling water and infuse for 3 minutes.

Add 4 cups of cold water to the pitcher and stir vigorously with a wooden spoon, smashing the peach pieces to a pulp.

Remove the pit from the remaining peach and cut it into six wedges, leaving the peach unpeeled. Combine the wedges in a serving pitcher with 4 cups of ice. Put another 4 cups of ice in a large sieve and place it over the serving pitcher. Strain the peach and tea infusion through the ice-filled sieve into the pitcher. Add peach syrup to taste and stir to mix. Serve immediately. The remaining syrup can be served with the iced tea for those who prefer their tea sweeter.

MINIATURE BERRY MUFFINS

Adding a cupful of chopped blueberries, cranberries, raspberries,
or strawberries to this versatile sweet muffin recipe is an easy way to create a batch
of freshly baked seasonal treats—perfect for breakfast or afternoon tea.

Makes 16 small or 8 regular muffins

2¼ cups pastry flour, sifted

¾ tablespoon baking powder

¾ cup sugar

¼ tablespoon salt

2 eggs

¾ cup milk

½ cup vegetable oil

1 cup chopped seasonal berries

Preheat the oven to 375°F. Butter a muffin tin.

In a large bowl, sift together the flour, baking powder, sugar, and salt.

In a medium bowl, combine the eggs, milk, and oil, and whisk to combine. Add the egg mixture to the dry ingredients and using an electric mixer, beat on low speed until thoroughly combined. Gently fold in the chopped berries.

Spoon the batter into the buttered muffin cups, filling them to the top. Bake for about 10 minutes, until the muffins have risen and are light gold on top.

A Summer Tea Party

Overnight guests often arrive at the White Barn Inn in the early afternoon, after several hours of traveling. An afternoon tea service featuring hot beverages, freshly baked scones, and sandwiches provides a revitalizing snack. Although the British drink hot tea even in summer, Americans usually prefer iced tea when it's hot outside. This menu offers several suggestions for chilled drinks spiked with fresh fruit.

RASPBERRY ICED TEA

Chefs are trained to do everything they can to add flavor to each recipe.
Here, in addition to dropping fresh berries into the tea, the chef extracts their essence
by simmering them in a sugar syrup before passing it through a sieve.
The syrup sweetens the tea and infuses it with the pure flavor of raspberries.
Try making this recipe with strawberries, too.

Makes 2½ quarts

1 cup sugar

Juice of ½ lemon

1 cup fresh raspberries, gently rinsed and drained

4 tablespoons English Breakfast tea leaves

In a medium saucepan, combine the sugar with 1 cup of water and bring to a boil over high heat. Continue to cook over medium heat, stirring to dissolve the sugar. When the sugar is dissolved, add the lemon juice and remove from heat.

In the jar of a blender, combine the sugar syrup and $\frac{1}{2}$ cup of raspberries and purée until smooth. Strain through a sieve and reserve in a small pitcher.

In a kettle, bring 4 cups of water to a boil. Place the tea leaves and half of the remaining raspberries in a heat-resistant pitcher. Add the boiling water and infuse for 3 minutes.

Add 4 cups of cold water to the raspberry tea and stir vigorously with a wooden spoon, smashing the raspberries to a pulp.

Combine the remaining raspberries in a serving pitcher with 4 cups of ice. Put another 4 cups of ice in a large sieve and place it over the serving pitcher. Strain the raspberry and tea infusion through the ice-filled sieve into the pitcher. Add raspberry syrup to taste and stir to mix. Serve immediately. The remaining syrup can be served with the iced tea for those who prefer their tea sweeter.

HOMEMADE LEMONADE

Not everyone wants to drink something caffeinated.
Lemonade is a refreshing and delicious alternative to iced tea.
For extra flavor, garnish this beverage with fresh mint.

Makes 4 cups

$\frac{1}{2}$ cup fresh lemon juice

$\frac{1}{2}$ cup sugar (or to taste)

1 cup ice

In a medium pitcher, combine the lemon juice and sugar with $2\frac{1}{2}$ cups of cold water and stir until the sugar dissolves. This mixture can be made a day ahead and refrigerated.

When ready to serve, add the ice to the pitcher of lemonade, stir, and serve immediately.

TOMATO AND CHEDDAR SANDWICHES

Heirloom tomatoes grown on farms in Maine have beautiful color
and a firm texture. One delicious way to eat tomatoes is simply to slice them,
sprinkle them with salt and pepper, and sandwich them between thin slices
of freshly baked bread with a slice of cheddar cheese.

Makes 6 finger sandwiches

4 slices white bread

4 slices cheddar cheese

2 ripe tomatoes, thinly sliced

Salt and freshly ground pepper

Place two slices of bread on a work surface. Layer two slices of cheddar cheese and several tomato slices on each piece of bread. Season with salt and pepper. Top with the remaining bread. Using a serrated knife, remove the crusts and slice each sand-wiche into three "fingers." Serve immediately.

COLD-SMOKED SALMON SANDWICHES

Makes 6 finger sandwiches

4 slices brown bread

1 tablespoon butter, softened

4 slices Cold-Smoked Salmon (see page 91)

Freshly ground pepper

Butter all four slices of bread on one side. Place two slices, buttered-side up, on a work surface. Cover each piece of bread with two salmon slices. Season with fresh-ly ground pepper, if desired. Top with the remaining slices of bread, buttered-side down. Using a serrated knife, remove the crusts and slice each sandwich into three "fingers." Serve immediately.

Egg Salad Sandwiches

*The addition of freshly cut chives or watercress brightens up the color
and adds another dimension of flavor to these satisfying little sandwiches.*

Makes 6 finger sandwiches

2 hard-cooked eggs, peeled

2 tablespoons Homemade Mayonnaise (see page 108),
or a good-quality commercial brand

Salt and freshly ground pepper

1 tablespoon chopped fresh chives or watercress (optional)

4 slices multigrain bread

In a medium bowl, mash the eggs with a fork. Add the mayonnaise. Continue mashing until the mixture forms a roughly textured paste. Season with salt and pepper. Add the chopped watercress or chives, if using.

Place two slices of bread on a work surface. Spread with the egg salad. Cover with the remaining slices of bread. Using a serrated knife, remove the crusts and slice each sandwich into three "fingers." Serve immediately.

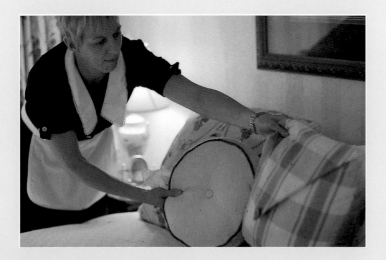

DOWN FEATHERBEDS AND COMFORTERS
AND A CHOICE OF PILLOWS TRANSFORM THE WHITE BARN
INN'S BEDS INTO IRRESISTIBLE NESTS. DRESSED
WITH COVERLETS AND THROWS IN DESIGNER FABRICS,
THEY ARE AS BEAUTIFUL TO BEHOLD AS THEY ARE
COMFORTABLE TO CURL UP IN.

SCONES WITH STRAWBERRY JAM

*Scones are among the easiest baked goods to make,
and berry preserves are simple to prepare, as well. Homemade preserves melt
right into the rich, fluffy heart of these fresh-from-the-oven scones.*

Makes 12 scones

3¼ cups all-purpose flour

½ cup sugar

1 teaspoon baking powder

¼ teaspoon baking soda

2¼ sticks cold unsalted butter

¾ cup buttermilk

½ cup dried currants

Strawberry Jam (see page 120)

Preheat the oven to 350°F. Butter a baking sheet.

In a large bowl, sift together the flour, sugar, baking powder, and baking soda. Cut in the butter to form coarse crumbs.

Add the buttermilk and currants and stir to combine. Cover with a damp cloth and allow the dough to rest in a cool place for 15 minutes.

Lightly flour a dry surface and rolling pin. Roll the dough out to a thickness of ½ inch. Using a 2-inch round cookie cutter, cut the dough into scones.

Place the scones on the buttered baking sheet. Bake for 15 minutes, until slightly risen and golden. Serve with Strawberry Jam.

STRAWBERRY JAM

*Nothing will make afternoon tea guests feel more special than a bowl
filled with just-made jam. This strawberry preserve is easy to make and can be
eaten as soon as it cools. Any remaining jam may be canned in glass jars,
following proper canning procedures, and stored for up to 6 months.*

Makes 1 quart

4 cups ripe strawberries, rinsed, cored, and quartered

3 cups sugar

Juice of 1 lemon

In a large saucepan with a heavy bottom, combine the strawberries, sugar,
and lemon juice. Bring to a boil over medium high heat. Reduce the heat to
medium low and simmer, uncovered, for 30 minutes, stirring occasionally,
until the mixture is reduced by half. Cool and serve, or can in glass jars
according to proper canning techniques.

DURING THE LATE SPRING, SUMMER,
AND FALL MONTHS, GUESTS MAY ENJOY REFRESHMENTS
OR LUNCHEON BY THE NEGATIVE-EDGE POOL
THAT BRIMS WITH WATER LIKE A FOREST POND. MASSAGES
AND OTHER SPA TREATMENTS ARE ALSO AVAILABLE
IN POOLSIDE CABANAS.

WARM BLUEBERRY
PETITS FOURS

*These little blueberry muffins are one of the best ways
to enjoy Maine's small, flavorful wild blueberries. They are best served warm,
when the blueberries are meltingly tender. Flexible muffin tins are best
for this recipe, which produces a soft-textured muffin.*

Makes 24 miniature muffins

7 eggs

2½ cups sugar

3 cups flour

4½ teaspoons baking powder

1 cup heavy cream

12 tablespoons (1½ sticks) unsalted
butter, melted

½ cup blueberries

Preheat the oven to 350°F. Butter two miniature muffin tins.

In a large bowl, beat the eggs with the sugar, using an electric mixer on high, for 6 minutes, until the mixture doubles in volume and the beater leaves a distinct trail when lifted from the batter.

In another large bowl, sift together the flour and baking powder. In a large measuring cup, combine the cream and the melted butter. Alternately fold the dry ingredients and the cream mixture into the beaten eggs, mixing only until all the ingredients are completely incorporated. Gently stir in the blueberries.

Spoon the batter into miniature muffin cups, filling them to the top. Bake for 10 minutes, until golden brown.

A Summer Seafood Dinner

Many diners at the White Barn Inn request the chef's recommendation for an all-seafood dinner featuring the best seasonal fish from Maine waters. This menu includes two fish that swim off the coast of Maine each summer—tuna and striped bass—as well as soft-shell crab, a specialty from Maryland's Chesapeake Bay.

TANDOORI-CRUSTED SOFT SHELL CRAB WITH AVOCADO AND LIME SALSA

This dish celebrates contrasting textures and flavors. The smooth coolness of the avocado-lime salsa sets off the crunch and spice of the soft shell crab. Tandoori powder, traditionally used on foods cooked in a tandoori oven, is an Indian spice mixture including dried and ground coriander, fenugreek, cumin, cayenne, nutmeg, and paprika or some other spice that produces a red color. It is available from Indian and international grocers, or by mail order from gourmet spice merchants.

Serves 4

1 cup milk

Salt, freshly ground pepper, and cayenne

4 jumbo soft-shell crabs, cleaned

2 ripe avocados

2 limes

1 cup plain yogurt

1 teaspoon crushed garlic

½ small cucumber, peeled, seeded, and diced

½ cup cornmeal

1 tablespoon tandoori powder

½ cup blended oil (see Note)

In a large bowl, combine the milk with a pinch of salt and pinch of cayenne. Place the crabs in the milk and refrigerate while preparing the rest of the ingredients.

Peel the avocados and cut the flesh into quarter-inch dice. Place the diced avocado in a medium bowl. Cut off the skin of the lime and dice the flesh. Add the diced lime and any juice to the avocado. Season to taste with salt, pepper, and cayenne.

In a medium bowl, combine the yogurt and crushed garlic. Stir in the cucumber and season with salt, pepper, and cayenne.

In a shallow bowl, combine the cornmeal and tandoori powder. In a large sauté pan, heat the oil over high heat. Remove the crabs from the milk and dredge them in the seasoned cornmeal. Place the crabs in the pan and sauté for about 3 minutes on each side, until golden brown.

To serve, place some avocado and lime salsa in the center of each of four plates. Drizzle the yogurt mixture around the outside of each plate. Place the crabs on top of the salsa.

Note: Blended oil is a mixture of 90 percent vegetable oil and 10 percent olive oil.

GRILLED YELLOWFIN TUNA LOIN
ON SUMMER CORN AND SHELLFISH HASH WITH
SMOKED TOMATO COULIS

Both bluefin and yellowfin tuna are caught in Maine waters.
Chef Cartwright prefers yellowfin tuna for this dish because its firm flesh
holds up well on the grill. Start by smoking the tomatoes for the coulis.
While the tomatoes are smoking, make the shellfish hash. You can reheat
the hash and the coulis while grilling the tuna.

Serves 4

1½ pounds yellowfin tuna loin, cut into 4 steaks

1 tablespoon extra-virgin olive oil

Salt and freshly ground pepper

Summer Corn and Shellfish Hash (see page 126)

Smoked Tomato Coulis (see page 128)

Preheat a charcoal grill to high.

Coat the tuna steaks with olive oil and season with salt and pepper. Place the tuna on the grate of the grill directly over the heat and cook for 2 to 3 minutes on each side for medium rare.

To serve, spoon some Summer Corn and Shellfish Hash in the center of each of four plates. Using a sharp knife, cut each tuna steak in half and arrange the two halves on each plate on top of the hash. Drizzle the Smoked Tomato Coulis over the tuna and the hash.

Summer Corn and Shellfish Hash

Serves 4

3 tablespoons blended oil (see Note)

½ medium onion, diced

1 sprig fresh thyme

1 cup dry, fruity white wine, such as sauvignon blanc

16 littleneck clams, scrubbed under cool running water

16 Maine mussels, scrubbed under cool running water

2 small potatoes, peeled and cut into quarter-inch dice

1 teaspoon butter

Kernels from 2 ears young white corn

4 large sea scallops, cut into quarters

In a sauté pan large enough to hold the clams, heat 1 tablespoon of oil over high heat. Add a third of the diced onion, half the thyme sprig, $\frac{1}{2}$ cup of white wine, and the clams. Cover and cook for 4 to 5 minutes over high heat, until the clams open. Remove the pan from the heat and allow to cool.

In a sauté pan large enough to hold the mussels, heat 1 tablespoon of oil over high heat. Add a third of the diced onion, the remaining thyme sprig, the remaining white wine, and the mussels. Cover and cook for 4 to 5 minutes over high heat, until the mussels open. Remove the pan from the heat and allow to cool.

Remove the clams and mussels from the pan juices, remove the meat, and discard the shells. Combine the pan juices and strain through a fine sieve lined with cheesecloth into a bowl.

In a large sauté pan, heat the remaining oil over high heat. Add the remaining diced onion and the diced potatoes. Cook over high heat for 2 to 3 minutes, until the potatoes are lightly browned. Reduce the heat to medium and add the butter and corn kernels. Cook, stirring, for 2 minutes. Add the strained shellfish pan juices and cook over medium heat for 8 to 10 minutes, until the potatoes and corn are tender and the liquid has reduced to a thick sauce that clings to the vegetables. Add the scallops, clams, and mussels and cook over medium heat for 1 minute. Season with salt and pepper and remove from the heat.

Note: Blended oil is a mixture of 90 percent vegetable oil and 10 percent olive oil.

Smoked Tomato Coulis

Makes about 1½ cups

Wood chips for smoking,
such as hickory, maple, or apple

8 ripe tomatoes

1 sprig fresh basil

1 tablespoon blended oil (see Note)

½ medium onion, diced

1 cup V-8 juice

Salt and freshly ground pepper

Light two handfuls of wood chips in the bottom of a charcoal grill. Cut the tomatoes in half and place them skin-side down on the grill grate over the wood chips. Cover the grill, leaving a small gap or adjusting the chimney in a slightly open position, and smoke the tomatoes for 20 minutes.

Remove the leaves from the sprig of basil. Reserve four leaves, cutting them into fine julienne, to garnish the finished dish.

In a medium saucepan, combine the blended oil, stem and remaining leaves of basil, and diced onion. Cook for 5 minutes, until the onion is translucent but not brown. Add the smoked tomatoes and V-8 juice and bring to a boil over medium high heat. Reduce the heat to medium low and simmer for 10 minutes, until the tomatoes break down and the sauce thickens.

Purée the sauce in a food processor. Strain through a fine sieve into a bowl, discarding the seeds and skins, and season the coulis with salt and pepper.

Note: Blended oil is a mixture of 90 percent vegetable oil and 10 percent olive oil.

Strawberry, Mandarin Orange, and Champagne Soup

*This soup can be prepared earlier in the day and finished with the addition
of the chilled champagne at the last minute. If you can't find mandarin orange purée
at a gourmet store or through a catalog, you can substitute 2 cups of
pulpy orange juice, preferably from mandarin oranges*

Makes 5 cups

2 cups mandarin orange purée

1 cup cored and chopped strawberries

1 cup white dessert wine, such as muscat

4 sprigs fresh mint

1 cup champagne, chilled

In a blender combine the mandarin orange purée, strawberries, white wine, and
mint. Purée until smooth. Strain through a fine sieve into a bowl or pitcher, cover,
and refrigerate. Just before serving, stir in the chilled champagne.

TO CREATE PRESENTATIONS THAT CELEBRATE EACH SEASON,
FINE PRODUCTS ARE FLOWN IN FROM
AROUND THE COUNTRY TO COMPLEMENT LOCALLY
GROWN FRUIT AND VEGETABLES. PLUMP MANDARIN ORANGES
GIVE SPARKLE TO SUMMER'S COLD SOUPS,
SORBETS, AND BEVERAGES.

PAN-ROASTED STRIPED BASS AND LOBSTER RAVIOLI WITH SUMMER ZUCCHINI RIBBONS AND SAFFRON FOAM

*Striped bass is a robust game fish with a beautiful skin
that turns crisp when pan-roasted, adding extra taste and texture
to this dish. With thinly sliced ribbons of squash, lightly sautéed
baby spinach, and a saffron-colored sauce, this fish entrée is full of
fresh summer flavors and colors. For additional appeal,
we garnish this dish with lobster oil and fried shallots
at the White Barn Inn.*

Serves 4

2 medium zucchini

2 medium yellow squash

3 tablespoons plus 2 teaspoons unsalted butter

1 shallot, diced

1 cup champagne

Pinch of saffron (about 20 threads)

1 cup heavy cream

Salt, freshly ground pepper, and cayenne

2 drops fresh lemon juice

1 pound striped wild bass, cut into 4 filets

4 cups baby spinach, stemmed and rinsed

2 tablespoons olive oil

4 Lobster Ravioli (see page 133), cooked

Cut the zucchini and yellow squash in half lengthwise. Using a mandoline or Asian vegetable slicer, cut both vegetables into thin, long, ribbonlike slices about ½ inch wide.

In a medium sauté pan, heat 2 tablespoons of the butter over medium heat. Add the diced shallot and sauté for 1 minute, until translucent.

Stir in the saffron and ¾ cup champagne and cook over medium high heat until reduced by half. Reduce the heat to medium and add the cream. Cook for 5 minutes, until the sauce coats the back of a spoon. Strain through a fine sieve, season to taste with salt, pepper, cayenne, and lemon juice, and set aside

Heat a large sauté pan over medium high heat. Place the bass, skin-side down, in the dry, hot pan and sear for 3 to 4 minutes, until the skin becomes crisp. Reduce the heat to medium and add 1 teaspoon of butter to the pan. When the butter turns a rich brown, turn the filets and reduce the heat to low. Cook for 5 minutes.

In a large sauté pan over medium high heat, melt 1 teaspoon of butter. Add the spinach and cook, tossing gently, for 2 minutes or until wilted. Set aside in a warm place.

In a clean sauté pan over medium heat, melt the remaining tablespoon of butter. Add the squash ribbons and cook for 2 minutes, stirring gently, until tender. Set aside in a warm place.

Reheat the sauce over high heat. Add the remaining champagne and bring to a boil.

To serve, place the squash ribbons on one side of each of four dinner plates (oval plates are best, if available). Place the spinach on the other side of the plate. Top the squash with the bass filet. Top the spinach with the ravioli. Using a hand-held blender, beat the sauce until it foams. Spoon the foam and sauce on top of the fish and ravioli, and serve at once.

Lobster Ravioli

Ravioli can be made up to six weeks ahead of time and frozen.
Since the Pan-Roasted Striped Bass recipe calls for only four ravioli, the remaining
ravioli can be enjoyed in a separate meal. One of my favorite light dinners
is a bowl of lobster bisque garnished with a raviolo, as a single ravioli is called.

Makes 8 to 10 3-inch ravioli

FILLING

¼ pound salmon filet

1 tablespoon salt

¼ cup heavy cream

2 tablespoons diced cooked lobster meat

1 tablespoon lobster roe

1 teaspoon chopped fresh parsley

Freshly ground pepper and cayenne

In the bowl of a food processor, combine the salmon and salt and pulse to combine. With the motor running, slowly add the cream. Stop processing when the cream is incorporated into the salmon. Add the lobster, lobster roe, and parsley and season with pepper and cayenne. Pulse a few times until the lobster is incorporated and the mixture has a rough, pastelike consistency.

RAVIOLI

1¾ cups bread flour or
all-purpose flour

6 egg yolks

2 tablespoons olive oil

1 pinch salt

1 tablespoon milk

In the bowl of a food processor, combine the flour, 5 egg yolks, olive oil, and salt. Pulse for 30 seconds, or until the mixture has the texture of wet sand. Turn the mixture out onto a work surface and knead it with the palms of your hands to form a dough. Continue kneading the dough until it is smooth and pliable. Gather it up loosely into a ball, cover with plastic wrap, and let it rest for 30 minutes in the refrigerator.

Make an egg wash by beating together the remaining egg yolk and the milk in a small bowl.

Lightly flour a work surface and rolling pin (or put the dough in a pasta machine on the #1 setting). If rolling by hand, roll the dough as thinly as possible into a rectangular sheet roughly 12 by 14 inches.

Brush the entire sheet of pasta with the egg wash. Cut the sheet in half lengthwise, leaving both pieces on the work surface. Working down the edge of one sheet, place one tablespoon of the lobster filling 2 inches in from the side and top. Place another tablespoon of filling 4 inches below this. Repeat this step until you reach the bottom of the sheet. Make another vertical row of filling 4 inches from the first row. Repeat until you have used all the lobster filling to create evenly spaced portions on the sheet of pasta.

Fold the second sheet of pasta over the sheet with the filling. Press down to seal the pasta around the filling.

Using a 3-inch fluted cutter, cut round ravioli, making sure the edges are fully sealed.

The ravioli can be placed on a baking sheet and frozen. Store the frozen ravioli in an airtight container or zipper-lock bag for up to six weeks.

To cook the ravioli, bring a large pot of salted water to a boil. Drop the ravioli in the boiling water. As soon as the water returns to a boil, reduce the heat to medium. Fresh ravioli will cook in 2 minutes; frozen ravioli will take 5 to 6 minutes. The ravioli is done when the pasta and filling are tender. Remove the cooked ravioli with a slotted spoon.

A Selection
of Summer Sorbets

Sorbets keep nicely in the freezer for several days. You can make this selection of fruit sorbets earlier in the week and delight your guests with a multicolored dessert. Or just serve a single sorbet garnished with a mint sprig or edible flower for an equally delightful finish to the meal. These recipes call for fruit purée, which is available from specialty stores. If you can't find fruit purée, you can make it by stewing a mixture of fruit and sugar over low heat until the fruit breaks down. Purée the fruit in a food processor and pass it through a sieve to remove any seeds or fibers. To calculate the correct ratio of fruit and sugar, you'll need a kitchen scale to weigh the fruit. Then add enough sugar to equal one-tenth the weight of the fruit.

GRIOTTE SORBET

*A griotte is a dark, sour cherry, similar to the cherries
used to make the famous Black Forest cake of Germany.
Bing cherries may be substituted, but they may be
too sweet. A better choice is Early Richmond
or Montmorency cherries.*

Makes 2½ quarts

1½ cups sugar

5 cups griotte purée

In a large saucepan, combine the sugar with 2 ¾ cups water and bring to a boil, stirring until the sugar is dissolved.

Place the purée in a large bowl. Pour the hot sugar syrup over the purée and stir well to blend. Let cool to room temperature. Freeze in an ice cream machine, following the manufacturer's instructions.

APRICOT SORBET

Makes about 2 quarts

1¾ cups sugar

4 cups apricot purée

In a large saucepan, combine the sugar with 2 cups of water and bring to a boil, stirring until the sugar is dissolved.

Place the purée in a large bowl. Pour the hot sugar syrup over the purée and stir well to blend. Let cool to room temperature. Freeze in an ice cream machine, following the manufacturer's instructions.

BLUEBERRY SORBET

Makes about 2 quarts

1¾ cups sugar

3¼ cups blueberry purée

In a large saucepan, combine the sugar with 1¾ cups water and bring to a boil, stirring until the sugar is dissolved.

Place the purée in a large bowl. Pour the hot sugar syrup over the purée and stir well to blend. Let cool to room temperature. Freeze in an ice cream machine, following the manufacturer's instructions.

STRAWBERRY CHAMPAGNE SORBET

Makes 2½ quarts

3 cups sugar

2 cups champagne

2 cups strawberry purée

In a large saucepan, combine the sugar with 1 cup of champagne and 2 cups of water. Bring to a boil, stirring until the sugar is dissolved.

Place the purée in a large bowl. Pour the hot sugar syrup over the purée and stir well to blend. Stir in the remaining cup of champagne. Let cool to room temperature.

Freeze in an ice cream machine, following the manufacturer's instructions. Because this sorbet includes alcohol, which slows the freezing process, it will be necessary to run the ice cream machine a few minutes longer than with the other sorbets.

A Summer Cocktail

WATERMELON COSMOPOLITAN

*This beverage translates watermelon's irresistible flavor
and color into a refreshing cocktail.*

Makes 2 cocktails

4 ounces vodka

⅓ cup crushed, seeded watermelon

¾ ounce watermelon schnapps

¾ ounce freshly squeezed lime juice

1 ounce triple sec

2 small wedges watermelon, for garnish

Chill two large martini glasses. In a cocktail shaker, combine all of the
ingredients and add crushed ice. Shake, then strain into chilled martini
glasses. Garnish with a small wedge of watermelon.

Summer Ingredients

CORN

Corn changes color and flavor throughout the growing season. The first summer corn is light in color, sweet, and succulent. Grilled on the cob then cut into kernels, it makes a delicious cold salad.

BLUEBERRIES

If you ask anyone from Maine, they will tell you that Maine wild blueberries are the best in the world. Sweet and juicy, they grow only during a five-week season from mid-July to late August.

STRAWBERRIES

Strawberries are harvested throughout the summer months in Maine. Full of flavor and firmly textured, they are delicious served in uncomplicated fruit salads and also form the basis for intense purées that can flavor sorbets, iced teas, and soups.

RED PEPPERS

Ranging in flavor from sweet to spicy, these versatile vegetables add colorful highlights to cooked and raw preparations. They also hold up well on the grill. Cooked and puréed, they make a brightly colored coulis to serve with fish and meat dishes.

TOMATOES

Brightly colored and filled with flavorful juice, the tomato is the ultimate summer vegetable. Harvested from July until the first frost, locally grown varieties include a number of heirloom tomatoes that vary widely in color, flavor, and shape.

SQUASH

Mild-tasting, firm-textured, and varied in color and shape, squash is the perfect foil for light summer sauces and an ideal garnish for grilled meats and fish. Varieties including zucchini, yellow squash, and pattypan are plentiful throughout the summer.

CHERRIES

After Maine's cherry trees bloom in spring, they prepare for a brief summertime harvest that is welcomed with a burst of pie-making and canning.

Autumn at the
WHITE BARN INN

Autumn arrives quietly in Maine before gathering force to explode in a colorful crescendo by mid-October. In the last days of August or early September, the sky begins to burn a brighter, deeper blue. The sun sets with a redder glow and darkness descends a little earlier each day, with a chill that calls for sweaters and wood-burning fires. One morning waves gently lick the sand at Gooch's Beach into a silver sheen. The next day dawns with the sound of heavy surf pounding the shore, shooting geysers of foam high into the air. Shreds of red seaweed scuttle like bits of torn lace along the breezy beach, and the wind teases leaves from trees that have begun to trade their summer green for fiery autumn hues.

Masses of seaweed and moss that hug the rocks along Ocean Avenue turn gold overnight, glowing with a burnished light against the brown-black stone. Wildflowers and grasses along country roads fade and go to seed, creating a tapestry of deeply varied brown interwoven with spiked pods and silky puffs adorned with tiny seeds. The trees succumb to autumn's pull, their tips turning red, maroon, and gold, then blush slowly downward until they stand like towering candles in full flame. At its peak autumn ignites the forests and fields into a pulse-quickening conflagration that burns through the countryside, leaving behind the rustling of dead leaves and the sharp scent of autumn bonfires.

With its clear light and warm afternoons, autumn is the perfect season for the year's final boat outings. The view of the bright tree-lined shore from across the waves is one of Maine's finest prospects, and the cool fall waters produce a plentiful harvest. Mussels, oysters, clams, and lobsters grow firm and sweet in the cold autumn waters. The woods and skies offer up a harvest feast, with turkey, duck, and venison satisfying the season's hunger for flavorful game. Within the woods knowledgeable foragers scan the forest floor, searching for cèpes, hen-of-the-woods, and oyster mushrooms that thrive in fall's cooler, moister climate. Along the roadsides farm stands contribute to the harvest mood with their bright displays of pumpkins, butternut and acorn squash, baskets of crisp apples and pears, and jugs of just-pressed cider.

In the kitchen of the White Barn Inn, Chef Cartwright plans menus that celebrate autumn's rich colors and mellow flavors. For a vegetarian offering, he creates a puff pastry bursting with tangy goat cheese and forest mushrooms. Served on a bed of tender greens and herbs, this hearty appetizer is followed by an entrée of ravioli filled with purees of butternut squash, roasted beets, and pesto-flavored potatoes that echo the colors of the autumn landscape. Whole steamed lobster, shelled and

ish their celebration with pumpkin pie, the chef opens his menu with pumpkin, featured in a delicately flavored, velvety soup. It is followed by a salad dressed with pumpkinseed oil and spiked with Roquefort and spice-dusted pecans. Such classics as cornbread stuffing and tart cranberry relish promise to satisfy the traditionalist, while Black Cherry and Kirsch Baked Alaska brings the meal to a stylishly retro close.

On the day after Thanksgiving, the chef transforms the excess from this feast into a delicious picnic menu to take along on a driving, walking, or cycling expedition.

On the day after Thanksgiving, the chef transforms the excess from this feast into a delicious picnic menu to take along on a driving, walking, or cycling expedition.

arranged atop a bed of fettuccine coated with cognac coral butter sauce is a signature dish served year-round at the White Barn Inn. It is especially delicious in fall when Maine lobsters are their sweetest and most succulent.

With a New England turkey dinner served throughout the afternoon and into the evening, Thanksgiving is the busiest day of the year at the White Barn Inn. The chef enjoys combining the traditional ingredients of the Thanksgiving feast with innovative preparations to surprise and delight his guests. While many Americans fin-

But for those whose idea of autumn pleasures is a cozy afternoon or evening spent inside by the fire, another menu celebrates the season's bounty with mushroom salad and a simple yet sophisticated shellfish ragout that can be enjoyed fireside. On a nostalgic note, the meal ends with s'mores—that addictive campfire favorite combining graham crackers (homemade this time), marshmallows (also homemade), and rich, dark chocolate. Accompanied by Irish coffee and hot mulled cider, this dessert promises to take the chill off even the coolest autumn evening.

AUTUMN MENUS

Thanksgiving Day Dinner

Pumpkin Soup with Seared Diver Scallops and Five-Spice Cream

An Autumn Assortment of Lettuces
in a Pumpkin Seed Vinaigrette with Roquefort Cheese
and Spiced Pecans

Roasted Maine Turkey with Sage and Onion Stuffing
and Gravy, Sweet Potato Hash, Cranberry Relish,
Brussels Sprouts with Sautéed Shallots, and Whipped Potatoes

Black Cherry and Kirsch Baked Alaska

•

Day after Thanksgiving
Driving Tour Picnic

Spiced Pumpkin Soup

Turkey Sandwich with Stuffing and Cranberry Relish

Belgium Endive and Frisée Salad with Maine Goat Cheese
and Grainy Mustard Vinaigrette

Butternut Squash Cookies

Fall Vegetarian Dinner

Local Forest Mushroom and New England Goat Cheese Pithiviers with
Arugula and Herb Salad with Chanterelle Vinaigrette

Roasted Red Pepper Sorbet

Ravioli of Butternut Squash, Roasted Beet,
and Pesto Potato on Spinach with Truffle Sauce

or

Steamed Maine Lobster Nestled on a Bed of Homemade Fettucine with
Carrot, Ginger, Snow Peas, and a Cognac Coral Butter Sauce

Poire William Crème Brûlée on a Sablé Biscuit and Pear Sorbet
with Spiced Port Wine Sauce

•

Romantic Fireside Dinner

Warm Fall Mushroom Salad with Sherry Vinaigrette

Ragout of Maine Salmon with Local Shellfish Medley
and Saffron Champagne Sauce

S'mores

Mulled Apple Cider

Irish Coffee

Thanksgiving Day Dinner

The tradition of the Thanksgiving Day feast began in New England, so it is an especially meaningful time in Maine for celebrating not only the history of the region, but also its natural bounty: pumpkins, potatoes, cranberries, and turkey. The colors of the meal are beautiful, and the flavors range from sweet to savory, with tart and spicy notes. Several of the dishes served for Thanksgiving at the White Barn Inn are American classics, including sage and cornbread stuffing, creamy whipped potatoes, and butter-basted turkey. But the pumpkin soup, garnished with a local scallop and a dollop of Asian-spiced whipped cream, is an unexpected way of integrating that most autumnal of squashes into the meal. A green salad tossed with pumpkinseed oil vinaigrette is garnished with crumbled Roquefort and spiced pecans. And baked Alaska, with its barely warmed meringue exterior and chilly center infused with cherries, kirsch, and chocolate, offers a beautiful surprise for dessert.

PUMPKIN SOUP WITH SEARED DIVER SCALLOPS AND FIVE-SPICE CREAM

*Simmered with cream and chicken broth (or vegetable stock,
for an equally savory vegetarian version), pumpkin makes an elegant soup
with a smooth texture and rich golden color. Maine shellfish is at its best
when the waters are cold, so diver-harvested scallops make an especially delicious
addition. Five-spice powder in the whipped cream introduces warm Asian flavors,
and the fried ginger garnish adds another dimension of taste and
texture to the bowl of steaming soup.*

Serves 8

2 tablespoons unsalted butter

4 heaping cups peeled, diced raw pumpkin

1 small onion, diced (about ¼ cup)

1 carrot, peeled and diced (about $\frac{1}{4}$ cup)

1 McIntosh apple, peeled and diced
(about 1 cup)

1 clove garlic

1 sprig fresh thyme

$\frac{1}{2}$ cup white wine

4 cups chicken stock

1 cup heavy cream

$\frac{1}{4}$ teaspoon ground nutmeg

$\frac{1}{8}$ teaspoon ground cinnamon

Salt and freshly ground pepper, to taste

2 teaspoons olive oil

8 diver-harvested scallops

Five-Spice Cream (see page 150)

Crispy Fried Ginger strips (see page 150)

In a stockpot with a heavy bottom, melt the butter over medium heat. Add the pumpkin, onion, carrot, apple, garlic, and thyme and reduce the head to low. Sauté for about 10 minutes, stirring occasionally. Increase the heat to medium and add the white wine. Cook until the wine nearly evaporates. Add the chicken stock and cook the soup at a low simmer, stirring occasionally, for 30 minutes, until all the vegetables are soft. Using a food processor or a hand-held blender, purée the soup and strain it through a fine sieve. Stir in the cream and season with the nutmeg, cinnamon, salt, and pepper.

Heat the olive oil in a medium nonstick skillet over high heat. Season the scallops with salt and pepper, and place in the hot oil. Sear until golden, turning once, about 2 minutes per side. The scallops will continue to cook in the hot soup. Remove the scallops from the pan and drain on paper towels to remove excess oil.

To serve, place a seared scallop in the center of each of eight shallow soup bowls and cover with the soup. Garnish with a dollop of Five-Spice Cream and a few Crispy Fried Ginger strips.

FIVE-SPICE CREAM

Makes 2 cups

1 cup heavy cream

1 teaspoon five-spice powder

Pinch salt

In a medium mixing bowl, combine the cream and five-spice powder
and whip until the mixture forms stiff peaks. Season to taste with salt.

CRISPY FRIED GINGER

Makes about 2 tablespoons

1 (2-inch) piece ginger root, peeled

3 cups blended oil or canola oil (see Note)

Pinch salt

Using a mandoline or an Asian vegetable slicer, slice down the length of the ginger
root to make several very fine slices. With a sharp chef's knife, cut the slices lengthwise into very thin julienne strips the size of a quartered wooden matchstick.

In a deep medium skillet, heat the oil to 350°F on a deep-fry thermometer.
Carefully drop the ginger strips into the oil and fry for 3 to 4 minutes, until golden-
brown. Using a slotted spoon, remove the ginger from the oil, shaking off any
excess, and drain on paper towels. Sprinkle lightly with salt while hot.

Note: Blended oil is a mixture of 90 percent vegetable oil and 10 percent olive oil.

An Autumn Assortment of Lettuces in a Pumpkin Seed Vinaigrette with Roquefort Cheese and Spiced Pecans

*Many of our local farmers are growing lettuces in greenhouses,
so we can still get fresh greens in the fall. Autumn greens are a little heartier
than summer ones. I like to serve endive in the fall, along with radicchio and arugula,
all of which add a sharp, slightly bitter flavor to salads. I combine these
with soft leaves of Boston or Bibb lettuce to balance the texture and flavor. I love the
taste of roasted pumpkin seeds in the fall. Pumpkinseed oil lends that same toasted,
nutty flavor to the vinaigrette. The best pumpkinseed oil comes from Austria
and is available in some gourmet stores. If you can't find it, substitute ¼ cup
extra-virgin olive oil and toss 2 tablespoons of toasted pumpkin seeds into the salad
with the dressing. Roquefort adds nice, creamy depth with a sharpness that stands
up well to the lettuces, while spiced pecans contribute fire and crunch.*

Serves 8

1 head radicchio

2 heads Belgian endive

1 small head curly endive

1 small bunch arugula

1 head Boston or Bibb lettuce

1 teaspoon Dijon mustard

¼ cup sherry vinegar

¼ cup extra-virgin olive oil

¼ cup pumpkinseed oil

Salt and freshly ground pepper, to taste

½ cup crumbled Roquefort cheese

1 cup Spiced Pecans (see page 152)

Wash and dry all the greens. Tear into bite-sized pieces and toss to combine. Wrap and refrigerate until ready to serve.

In a small mixing bowl, combine the mustard and vinegar. Gradually add the olive oil and the pumpkinseed oil, whisking until the mixture is emulsified. Season to taste with salt and pepper.

Place the greens in a large bowl and toss with the vinaigrette, using only enough dressing to coat the leaves lightly. Season with additional salt and pepper, if desired. Divide the salad among eight plates, sprinkle evenly with crumbled Roquefort, and top with Spiced Pecans. Any remaining dressing will keep tightly covered in the refrigerator for up to a month.

SPICED PECANS

If you like fiery flavors, increase the quantities of the spices called for in this recipe. It will make more nuts than you need to garnish the salad, but the remaining nuts make a wonderful appetizer to serve with drinks before dinner.

Makes 3 cups

2 tablespoons unsalted butter, melted

¾ pound whole shelled pecans (about 3 cups)

⅛ teaspoon cayenne pepper, or more to taste

⅛ teaspoon chili powder, or more to taste

⅛ teaspoon curry powder, or more to taste

⅛ teaspoon salt, or more to taste

⅛ teaspoon freshly ground black pepper,
or more to taste

Preheat the oven to 400°F.

Melt the butter in a large skillet over medium heat. Add the pecans, cayenne, chili powder, curry powder, salt, and pepper and toss to coat the nuts evenly with the butter and the spices.

Transfer the nuts to a baking sheet and toast for 1 to 2 minutes, until lightly browned and sizzling. Serve warm.

ROASTED MAINE TURKEY WITH
SAGE AND ONION STUFFING AND GRAVY

*Near the White Barn Inn, several local farms breed flavorful turkeys
for Thanksgiving. If you can't find a local turkey producer, purchase a fresh turkey
from your supermarket or butcher. The flavor and texture will be far superior
to that of a frozen turkey. Stuffing a quartered apple in the neck cavity provides added
moisture and subtle flavor from within during roasting, and basting the turkey with
plenty of butter helps ensure that the breast remains moist and tender.*

Serves 8, with plenty of leftovers

1 (15-pound) fresh turkey, dressed

1 McIntosh apple

Sage and Onion Stuffing (see page 155)

8 tablespoons (1 stick) unsalted butter, at room temperature

2 tablespoons all-purpose flour

2 cups strong Turkey Stock (see page 160)

Salt and freshly ground pepper

Preheat the oven to 400°F.

Season the turkey inside and out with salt and pepper and place on a rack in a deep roasting pan. Cut the apple into quarters and place in the neck cavity. Loosely pack the main cavity with Sage and Onion Stuffing. Place the remaining stuffing in a buttered baking dish and cover with aluminum foil.

Rub the turkey breast with the butter. Pour 1 cup of water into the bottom of the roasting pan and place the pan in the preheated oven. Bake for 20 minutes, baste the turkey with the pan juices, and return it to the oven. Bake for another 10 minutes, checking to make sure that the breast is not getting too dark. Baste with pan juices and return to the oven, reducing the heat to 325°F. Cook for a total of 3 hours, or until the turkey reaches an internal temperature of 160°F on a meat thermometer. Continue basting with pan juices every 20 minutes, checking periodically to make sure the breast is not getting too browned. If the breast and legs start to turn dark brown, cover them with a loose tent of aluminum foil, and continue baking and basting.

About 1 hour before the turkey is fully cooked, place the baking dish of stuffing in the oven. Fifteen minutes before removing the turkey from the oven, remove the aluminum foil (if used) from the breast and legs and the pan of stuffing, and allow both to brown lightly.

Remove the turkey from the oven. Lift it from the pan and transfer it to a large serving platter or a carving board with a channel to collect any juices.

To make the gravy, sprinkle the flour over the pan juices, scraping up any browned bits from the bottom of the pan, and whisk to dissolve any lumps. Place the pan in a hot oven and roast for 5 minutes. Remove from the oven and place on the stovetop over medium heat. Slowly whisk in the Turkey Stock. Transfer the gravy to a saucepan and cook over low heat for 15 minutes. Skim off any fat that rises to the surface and season with salt and pepper to taste. Strain through a fine sieve into a gravy boat and serve hot.

SAGE AND ONION STUFFING

This stuffing is made with homemade cornbread.
The recipe that follows makes a dry cornbread that is not
suitable for eating by itself but is perfect for absorbing
all the butter and turkey stock that flavors it so richly.
Sage adds a subtle herbal note.

Serves 8, with leftovers

1 cup (2 sticks) unsalted butter

1 cup diced onion

¼ cup chopped fresh sage

1 cup milk

1 cup Turkey Stock (see page 160,
or use a good-quality canned chicken stock)

3 heaping cups crumbled, dried Cornbread for Stuffing
(see page 156)

2 large eggs, beaten

Salt and freshly ground pepper

Preheat the oven to 350°F.

In a skillet with a heavy bottom, melt the butter over medium heat. Add the onion and sauté until soft and translucent but not browned. Add the sage and remove from the heat.

Combine the milk and stock in a saucepan and bring to a boil over medium heat. Remove from the heat as soon as it boils.

Place the crumbled Cornbread for Stuffing in a large bowl. Add the sautéed onion, beaten eggs, and the hot stock mixture. Stir to combine all the ingredients thoroughly. Season to taste with the salt and pepper.

Butter an 8-inch baking dish and fill with the stuffing. Cover with aluminum foil and bake for 45 minutes. Remove the foil to let the stuffing brown, and bake for 15 minutes longer.

1½ cups yellow cornmeal

1 cup all-purpose flour

1 tablespoon baking powder

1 teaspoon salt

1 cup milk

1 large egg, beaten

3 tablespoons unsalted butter, melted

Preheat the oven to 425°F.

Butter an 8-inch baking pan. In a large bowl, whisk together the cornmeal, flour, baking powder, and salt. In another bowl, whisk together the milk, egg, and butter. Add the wet ingredients to the dry ingredients, stirring just until combined.

Pour the batter into the prepared pan and bake on the center rack of the oven for 20 to 25 minutes, or until the top turns pale gold and a tester comes out clean. Cool the cornbread in the pan on a rack for 5 minutes. Remove from the pan and continue cooling on the rack until it reaches room temperature.

Coarsely crumble the cornbread into a large baking pan. Let it stand at room temperature, uncovered, for at least three hours or overnight, until it becomes slightly stale and hardened.

Preheat the oven to 300°F.

Place the pan of crumbled cornbread on the center rack of the oven and bake, stirring occasionally, until the crumbs are dried and golden, about 30 minutes.

SWEET POTATO HASH

Every year I experiment with recipes that use leftover turkey in creative ways.
This one was so delicious that I decided to make it part of my Thanksgiving Day menu.
Since the recipe calls for just 2 cups of dark meat (a little less than one leg
of a 15-pound turkey), you can easily cut off the meat required for this side dish
while carving the turkey. The moist hash makes a perfect accompaniment to a slice
of white meat. If you prefer, however, you can make it the day after Thanksgiving
and serve it with stuffing and cranberry relish. However you serve it,
it's a wonderful way to enjoy the rich and flavorful leg meat.

Serves 8

2 tablespoons blended oil (see Note)

2 tablespoons diced onion

1 clove garlic

1 tablespoon unsalted butter

2 cups diced, peeled sweet potatoes (about 2 medium potatoes)

2 cups diced cooked turkey leg meat

1 cup turkey gravy

½ cup Turkey Stock (see page 160)

In a medium saucepan heat the blended oil over medium heat. Add the onion and garlic and sauté until translucent but not browned. Add the butter and the diced sweet potatoes and continue cooking over medium low heat for 5 minutes, or until the potatoes begin to darken and soften on the outside (they will still be hard inside).

Add the turkey, gravy, and Turkey Stock and cook over low heat for about 20 minutes, or until the sweet potatoes are cooked through.

Note: Blended oil is a mixture of 90 percent vegetable oil and 10 percent olive oil.

CRANBERRY RELISH

Onion, port, and champagne vinegar add savory notes to this sweet-and-tart relish,
which is equally delicious served warm with hot turkey or other game,
or right from the refrigerator on day-after-Thanksgiving turkey sandwiches.

Makes 4 cups

1 pound fresh New England cranberries

2 teaspoons diced onion

1 cup sugar

½ cup port wine

¼ cup champagne vinegar

In the top of a large double boiler over medium heat, combine the cranberries, onion, sugar, port, and vinegar. Stir to combine and cover. Cook over simmering water for 45 minutes, stirring occasionally, until some of the cranberries pop, creating a thick, saucelike consistency. The relish will thicken as it cools. It may be stored in an airtight container in the refrigerator for one week.

AT THE WHITE BARN INN'S BAR, MURALS OF FARMYARD
ANIMALS RECALL THE STRUCTURE'S FORMER LIFE
AS A RUSTIC BARN, WHILE SHELVES OF THE FINEST SPIRITS
OFFER JUST ABOUT ANY REFRESHMENT
A GUEST MIGHT REQUEST.

TURKEY STOCK

Makes 3 cups

4 pounds roasted turkey bones

½ pound mixed aromatic vegetables,
such as carrots, leeks, onions, and celery, diced

1 clove garlic, crushed

12 sprigs fresh herbs, such as thyme, rosemary, and tarragon

1 cup dry white wine, such as Sauvignon Blanc

Preheat the oven to 450°F.

Place the bones in a large roasting pan and roast, turning occasionally, for 15 minutes, until golden brown. Add the vegetables to the pan and continue roasting for 5 minutes.

Transfer the bones and vegetables to a large stockpot and add the garlic, herbs, and white wine. Cover with water and bring to a boil over high heat, skimming off any impurities that rise to the surface. Reduce the heat to medium and simmer the stock for four hours, until reduced by half.

Strain the mixture through a fine sieve. For a further reduced stock suitable for sauces, simmer the strained stock over medium heat until it is reduced by half. Store in an airtight container in the refrigerator for up to three days or freeze in ice cube trays, transferring the cubes of frozen stock to zipper-lock bags for up to a month.

Brussels Sprouts
with Sautéed Shallots

I love every vegetable in the cabbage family,
including brussels sprouts, which make me think of
little whole cabbages. They are best cooked
until tender but not mushy, and tossed with plenty
of butter, salt, and pepper. Butter balances
the sharp flavor of sprouts and in this recipe,
sautéed shallots add a savory note.

Serves 8

1 pound brussels sprouts

Salt and freshly ground white pepper

2 tablespoons unsalted butter

2 large shallots, diced (about 3 tablespoons)

Bring a large pot of water to a boil and salt it generously. Add the sprouts and cook just until soft, but not mushy. Depending upon the age and size of the sprouts, this will take from 7 to 10 minutes. Drain the sprouts and cut them in half.

In a skillet with a heavy bottom, melt the butter over medium low heat. Add the shallots and cook for about 5 minutes, until softened but not browned.

Toss the sprouts with the shallots and the butter. Season to taste with salt and freshly ground white pepper.

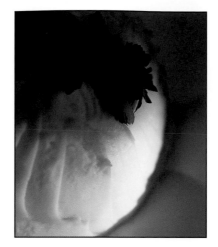

WHIPPED POTATOES

Many Americans are hesitant to use large quantities of butter, but it adds great flavor and texture to whipped potatoes. In fact, the more buttery and creamy whipped potatoes are, the better they taste. Thanksgiving only comes once a year, so why not take advantage of the occasion to enjoy a generous amount of butter?

Serves 8

4 Yukon gold potatoes, peeled and diced (about 4 heaping cups)

¾ cup (1½ sticks) unsalted butter

½ cup heavy cream

Salt and freshly ground pepper

Pinch freshly grated nutmeg (optional)

Preheat the oven to 300°F.

Bring a large pot of water to a boil and salt it generously. Add the potatoes and return to a boil. Reduce the heat to medium and simmer for 10 to 12 minutes, or until the potatoes are easily pierced by a fork. Drain the potatoes and place them on a baking sheet in the oven to dry for 5 minutes. Transfer the hot potatoes to a large bowl and mash until most of the lumps are removed.

In a medium saucepan with a heavy-bottom, combine the butter and cream over medium heat and warm until the butter is completely melted. Gradually add the cream mixture to the mashed potatoes and whisk until smooth. Season to taste with salt, pepper, and nutmeg, if desired. Serve immediately, or keep covered in a warm place until ready to serve.

Black Cherry and Kirsch Baked Alaska

*Baked Alaska is a visually stunning dessert that makes a fitting end
to a festive meal. The cool texture of the iced cream center hidden beneath a layer
of just-warmed meringue is a delightful surprise. Although this impressive dessert
does require several steps, it is surprisingly easy to reproduce at home.
If you prefer, substitute fresh berries for the black cherries.*

Serves 8

12 egg yolks

2¼ cups sugar

2 cups heavy cream

1 cup diced Chocolate Sponge (see page 165)

3 tablespoons kirsch

1 cup black sweet cherries (fresh, thawed if frozen, or canned)

1 cup egg whites (from about 6 large eggs)

In a medium heat-resistant bowl, combine the egg yolks and ½ cup of the sugar. Beat with an electric mixer on high speed until smooth and light yellow. Place the bowl over a pan of boiling water and cook, continuing to mix at high speed or by hand, for 4 to 5 minutes. The egg yolks will turn pale yellow and glossy. When the mixture forms a ribbon when dropped from the whisk (or when it reaches a temperature of 120°F on a candy thermometer), remove from the heat. Continue beating the mixture until it reaches room temperature.

In a medium bowl, whip the cream to form soft peaks. Fold the whipped cream into the cooled egg yolk mixture.

Cut the Chocolate Sponge into 1½-inch squares and drizzle the kirsch over them. Once the chopped cake has absorbed the kirsch, fold it into the whipped cream and egg mixture along with the black cherries. The cake will break up into the mixture. If you are using frozen or canned cherries, drain them before adding them to the mixture.

Butter a 20 x 3 x 2-inch log mold (also called a büche de Noël mold), then line it with plastic wrap, making sure that the lining is smooth and that no air bubbles are trapped between the plastic wrap and the mold. Pour the mixture into the mold, cover with plastic wrap, and freeze for at least 12 hours and up to 2 weeks.

After 12 hours, remove the frozen log from the mold, place on a heat-resistant serving platter, cover with plastic wrap, and return to the freezer.

Place the egg whites in a clean bowl with high sides. Using an electric mixer, whip the egg whites on medium speed until they start to foam. Add the remaining ¾ cup sugar. When the sugar is incorporated, whip the egg whites on high speed until they form stiff peaks.

Gently spoon the egg white mixture into a pastry bag fitted with a medium star tip. Remove the log from the freezer and pipe the mixture to cover it completely. Cover with plastic wrap and return the log to the freezer until ready to serve. It can be frozen at this point for up to 1 week.

To serve, preheat the broiler. Place the frozen, meringue-covered log on a baking sheet at least 6 inches below the heat source for just a few seconds, until the meringue is glazed and lightly browned. Watch carefully to avoid burning the meringue. Bring the whole Baked Alaska to the table and slice into individual servings.

Chocolate Sponge

Once it has cooled completely,
this airy cake can be wrapped tightly in plastic wrap
and stored in the refrigerator for 2 to 3 days or
in the freezer for up to a month.

Makes 1 (12 x 16-inch) cake

2 eggs

½ cup sugar

⅓ cup flour

2 tablespoons cornstarch

4 tablespoons dark cocoa powder

1 teaspoon baking powder

Preheat the oven to 375°F. Butter a 12 x 16-inch baking pan.

In a large bowl, combine the eggs with 2 tablespoons of cold water and beat with an electric mixer on high speed until foamy. Gradually add the sugar while continuing to mix.

Sift together the flour, cornstarch, cocoa, and baking powder. Carefully fold the dry ingredients into the egg yolk mixture until well combined.

Pour the batter into the prepared baking pan and bake for 15 minutes, or until a tester comes out clean. Turn the cake out onto a rack to cool.

Day after Thanksgiving
Driving Tour Picnic

The Friday after Thanksgiving can be a perfect time to work off some of the extra calories from the previous day's feast with an outdoor expedition. Fortunately, Thanksgiving dinner usually yields a plentiful array of excess from which to create delicious lunches and casual suppers. This simple picnic lunch, which features several dishes from the Thanksgiving Day menu, can be easily prepared and taken on a driving, biking, or walking tour.

SPICED PUMPKIN SOUP

Simply reheat yesterday's soup, or, for a spicier, richer first course, stir in any remaining Five-Spice Cream before packing this in a thermal container and heading for the outdoors.

Serves 4

4 cups Pumpkin Soup (see page 147)

¼ to ½ cup Five-Spice Cream (see page 150)

Salt and pepper

In a medium saucepan over medium low heat, reheat the soup. Stir in the leftover Five-Spice Cream, if using. Season to taste with salt and pepper. Transfer to a thermal container until ready to serve.

TURKEY SANDWICH WITH STUFFING
AND CRANBERRY RELISH

*One of the best ways to enjoy the remains of Thanksgiving dinner
is in a satisfying sandwich stacked high with sliced turkey,
a layer of cold stuffing, and a bright red garnish of cranberry relish.
The relish, savory with onion and vinegar, makes a deliciously
sweet-and-sour addition to a hearty fall sandwich.
If you are packing these sandwiches for a picnic, keep them cold
in a portable cooler, and add the cranberry relish just before
you are ready to eat them.*

Serves 4

8 slices firm-textured, seeded rye bread

2 tablespoons unsalted butter at room temperature (optional)

8 slices turkey, dark and white meat

Salt and freshly ground pepper

1 cup Sage and Onion Stuffing (see page 155)

1 cup Cranberry Relish (see page 159)

Spread four slices of bread lightly with butter, if using. Place two slices
of turkey on each slice of buttered bread and season to taste with salt
and pepper. Top with ¼ cup of stuffing and ¼ cup of cranberry relish.
Cover the sandwiches with the remaining bread slices, cut in half on the
diagonal, and serve.

Belgium Endive and Frisée Salad with Maine Goat Cheese and Grainy Mustard Vinaigrette

When shopping for the ingredients for this salad,
look for an aged goat cheese with a dry texture that will
crumble nicely. Good New England goat cheeses
to use include an aged crottin *from Vermont or*
a Blue Bonnet from Massachusetts.

Serves 4

2 heads frisée, dark outer leaves removed

1 head Belgian endive

1 bunch chives

1 teaspoon grainy Dijon mustard

¼ cup champagne vinegar

½ cup extra-virgin olive oil

4 tablespoons crumbled aged goat cheese

Salt and freshly ground pepper

Wash and dry the greens, tearing the pale, tender inner leaves of the frisée and cutting the endive leaves into bite-size pieces. Cover and refrigerate until ready to serve. Finely chop the lower portion of the chives, reserving the top 2½ inches of each chive for garnish.

Place the mustard in a small mixing bowl and whisk in the vinegar. Gradually add the oil, whisking to emulsify the dressing. Season to taste with salt and pepper.

Just before serving, place the greens in a large bowl. Add the crumbled goat cheese and chopped chives to the chilled greens. Dress lightly with vinaigrette, reserving any unused dressing in a covered container in the refrigerator for future use. Season the salad with salt and pepper, if necessary.

Divide the salad among four plates and garnish with the reserved chives.

BUTTERNUT SQUASH COOKIES

These cookies have a soft texture somewhere between that of a muffin and a cookie.
Butternut squash and pumpkin purée create a beautiful fall color and a surprising, mildly
sweet flavor. They are best when baked an hour or two before serving,
but the prepared dough can be shaped into a roll, wrapped tightly, and frozen for up
to two weeks. That way, you can cut cookies from the roll and bake as needed.

Makes 2 dozen

1 cup peeled, finely diced butternut squash

1¼ cups packed brown sugar

½ cup (1 stick) unsalted butter

2 eggs, beaten

½ teaspoon vanilla extract

1½ cups canned pumpkin purée

2½ cups all-purpose flour

4 teaspoons baking powder

½ teaspoon salt

½ teaspoon ground cinnamon

½ teaspoon ground nutmeg

½ cup chopped pecans (optional)

Preheat the oven to 350°F. Butter a baking sheet.

Bring a medium saucepan of salted water to a boil and add the squash. Cook for 5 minutes, or until fork-tender. Drain and reserve.

In a large bowl, cream the butter with the sugar until smooth. Add the eggs and beat thoroughly. Mix in the vanilla extract and pumpkin purée.

In another large bowl, whisk together the flour, baking powder, salt, cinnamon, and nutmeg. Combine the dry ingredients with the pumpkin mixture and stir just to combine. Stir in the diced squash and pecans, if using.

Drop well-rounded tablespoons of dough 2 inches apart on the buttered baking sheet.

Flatten each cookie slightly with the bottom of a glass that has been dipped in sugar.

Bake the cookies in the middle of the oven until lightly browned.

Fall Vegetarian Dinner

Many guests of the White Barn Inn stay for several days during peak leaf season to watch autumn unfold while sampling the offerings of the inn's kitchen. Often they will choose the vegetarian menu for dinner one night. This menu provides an excellent opportunity to celebrate the variety of seasonal vegetables. It features several dishes which can—and should—be made in advance, since it would be challenging for one person to prepare all the courses of this meal in a single day and still sit down to enjoy them with guests that night. If you prefer not to serve an entirely vegetarian menu, then substitute the lobster recipe on page 183 for the ravioli.

LOCAL FOREST MUSHROOM AND NEW ENGLAND GOAT CHEESE PITHIVIERS WITH ARUGULA AND HERB SALAD WITH CHANTERELLE VINAIGRETTE

For an appetizer full of variety in texture, color, and taste,
these buttery pithiviers—puff pastry pillows stuffed with tangy goat cheese
and sautéed mushrooms—are served warm with a salad of spicy arugula,
sweet Thai basil, and fresh parsley. If wild mushrooms are unavailable, substitute
a combination of cremini, white button, portobello, or oyster mushrooms. This recipe
can be easily made using the packaged frozen puff pastry sold in grocery stores.
The unbaked pithiviers can be assembled in advance and kept in an airtight
storage container in the freezer for up to 1 month.

Serves 4

1 tablespoon olive oil

1 tablespoon finely diced shallots

1 cup roughly chopped mixed wild mushrooms, such as chanterelle, chicken- and hen-of-the-woods, porcini, matsutake, or lobster mushrooms

1 pound frozen puff pastry, thawed

½ cup soft goat cheese, at room temperature

1 tablespoon chopped fresh herbs, such as chervil, chives, and parsley

1 egg, beaten

Preheat the oven to 350°F.

Heat the olive oil in a medium sauté pan over medium heat. Add the shallots and sauté for 1 to 2 minutes, until translucent but not browned. Add the mushrooms and sauté for 5 minutes, until tender. Season with salt and pepper and allow to cool.

On a clean, dry work surface, roll out a single ¼-inch layer of puff pastry. Using a 3-inch round cookie cutter, cut out eight pastry rounds.

In a medium bowl, combine the cooled mushrooms with the goat cheese and herbs, seasoning to taste with salt and pepper. Place a heaping tablespoon of the mushroom mixture in the center of four of the pastry rounds.

Lightly brush the outsides of the cheese-topped rounds with the beaten egg. Top with the remaining four rounds of puff pastry, pressing the edges to seal in the mixture. Brush the top of each pithivier with beaten egg. Using a sharp knife, lightly score the top of each pastry in a pinwheel pattern (the lines should be approximately ¼ inch apart on the outer edges of the circle).

Place on a buttered baking sheet and bake in the preheated oven for 10 to 12 minutes, until the pastry has risen and turned golden-brown. Serve at once with Arugula and Herb Salad with Chanterelle Vinaigrette (recipe follows).

The pithiviers can also be frozen on a baking sheet and stored in an airtight container in the freezer for up to a month before baking. If freezing, do not brush the pithiviers with egg wash. Defrost for ½ hour before baking, brush with egg wash, and bake for about 15 minutes, until puffed and golden brown.

ARUGULA AND HERB SALAD
WITH CHANTERELLE VINAIGRETTE

If you can't find Thai basil or chervil,
substitute cilantro for an equally refreshing mix of greens.
Oyster mushrooms, portobello, or even
white button mushrooms may be substituted
for the fresh chanterelles.

Serves 4

1 cup arugula

1 bunch fresh Thai basil

1 bunch flat-leaf parsley

1 bunch fresh chervil

2 ripe tomatoes

10 tablespoons olive oil

1 tablespoon diced shallots

½ cup sliced chanterelle mushrooms

4 tablespoons champagne vinegar

Salt and freshly ground pepper, to taste

Rinse and dry the arugula and fresh herbs, removing any yellowed leaves. Cover and refrigerate until ready to serve.

Bring a small saucepan of water to a boil and add the whole tomatoes. Blanch for 30 seconds to 1 minute, just until the skins start to split. Transfer to a bowl of cold water. When cool, remove the skins, seed the tomatoes (discarding the seeds and juice, or reserving to add to stocks, if desired), and cut the flesh into ⅛-inch dice.

In a medium skillet, heat 1 tablespoon of the olive oil over medium heat. Add the shallots and cook for 1 minute, until translucent but not browned. Add the chanterelles and cook for 5 minutes, until tender. Stir in the vinegar and season to taste with salt and pepper.

Pour the mushroom mixture into a fine sieve, reserving the pan juices in a small bowl. Gradually whisk the remaining olive oil into the juices to create an emulsion.

Combine the cooked mushrooms and the diced tomatoes, seasoning to taste with salt and pepper.

Gently toss the arugula and fresh herbs with a small amount of the dressing and a few spoonfuls of the mushroom-and-tomato mixture. Divide the salad among four plates. Arrange the remaining mushroom-and-tomato mixture around the outer edge of each plate. Place one hot pithivier next to the salad greens, and drizzle a small amount of the vinaigrette over the plate. Serve at once.

CHANTERELLE MUSHROOMS

THE FRESHEST SEASONAL INGREDIENTS, PAINSTAKINGLY PREPARED,
FORM THE BASIS FOR EACH DISH AT THE WHITE BARN INN. FOREST MUSHROOMS,
JUST HARVESTED THAT MORNING, ARE CAREFULLY SCRAPED TO REMOVE
THE STEMS' OUTSIDE COATING BEFORE BEING COOKED WHOLE.

ROASTED RED PEPPER
SORBET

*This sorbet has an amazing vermilion color and
an equally surprising taste that combines the sweet, tangy,
and slightly spicy flavors of roasted red peppers.
Serve it to your guests in chilled bowls while you slip back
into the kitchen to finish preparing the ravioli (or lobster) entrée.
You will be sure to hear exclamations of delight
when you return to the table.*

Makes 2 cups

½ cup sugar

1 cup Roasted Red Pepper Purée (see page 177)

Pinch salt

Pinch freshly ground pepper

In a medium saucepan, combine 1 cup of water and the sugar and cook over high heat, stirring occasionally, until the sugar dissolves. Place the Red Pepper Purée in a large bowl and stir in the hot syrup until combined. Season with a pinch of salt and pepper and let cool.

Freeze the mixture in an ice cream machine, following the manufacturer's instructions. Serve at once, or store in a covered container in the freezer for up to one day in advance.

ROASTED RED PEPPER PURÉE

*This purée can be prepared up to four days
in advance and refrigerated.*

Makes 1 cup

6 red bell peppers, halved and seeded

1 tablespoon sunflower oil

¼ cup water

Preheat the oven to 350°F.

Place the peppers in a glass baking dish large enough to hold them in a single layer. Pour the oil over the peppers and toss to coat well. Cover the baking dish with aluminum foil and roast for 30 minutes, until the peppers are soft but have not yet begun to brown.

Transfer the peppers to the bowl of a food processor, adding ¼ cup water. Purée until smooth. Pass the purée through a fine sieve to remove any pieces of skin.

Ravioli of Butternut Squash, Roasted Beet, and Pesto Potato on Spinach with Truffle Sauce

*The firm, supple sheets of pasta used to make ravioli may
be rolled out by hand or in a pasta machine.
For best results, use blended flour, a mixture of equal parts
bread flour, made from hard, glutinous wheat, and cake or pastry flour,
made from soft wheat. Sift the flour before measuring to ensure
the proper ratio of ingredients. Since egg yolks vary widely
in size, be sure to measure the yolks in a
measuring cup before adding them to the flour.*

Serves 4

RAVIOLI FILLINGS

½ pound Yukon Gold potatoes
(about 2 small potatoes),
peeled and diced

4 tablespoons (½ stick) unsalted butter

5 tablespoons olive oil

Salt and freshly ground pepper

2 tablespoons Pesto (see page 36)

½ pound butternut squash
(about ½ medium squash),
peeled and diced

Pinch freshly ground nutmeg

½ pound beets (about 2 medium beets),
washed, left whole with skin on

1 tablespoon olive oil

RAVIOLI

1¾ cups blended flour, sifted

½ cup lightly beaten egg yolks
(5 to 7 yolks from large eggs)

2 tablespoons olive oil

1 pinch fine salt

Truffle Cream Sauce (see page 181)

To make the fillings: Preheat the oven to 300°F.

Place the diced potatoes in a medium saucepan, cover with water, and bring to a boil over high heat. Reduce the heat to medium and cook until the potatoes can be easily pierced with a fork, 12 to 15 minutes. Drain the potatoes and place them on an ungreased baking sheet in the oven to dry for 5 minutes. Transfer the potatoes to a mixing bowl and mash until smooth, adding the butter and 4 tablespoons of olive oil. Season to taste with salt and freshly ground pepper. Set aside until ready to fill the ravioli. Just before filling them, add 2 tablespoons of Pesto to the potatoes and mix well.

Place the squash in a medium saucepan, cover with water, and bring to a boil over high heat. Reduce the heat to medium and cook until the squash is easily pierced with a fork, 7 to 9 minutes. Drain the squash cubes and place them on an ungreased baking sheet in the oven to dry for 5 minutes. Transfer to the bowl of a food processor and purée until smooth. Season to taste with salt, pepper, and a small pinch of nutmeg.

Increase the oven heat to 350°F. Rub the beets with the tablespoon of olive oil, season with salt and pepper, and wrap tightly in aluminum foil. Place in a baking dish and roast for 30 minutes, or until very tender when gently squeezed.

Remove the beets from the foil, cool, and peel. Dice the beets coarsely and place them in the bowl of a food processor. Purée until smooth, seasoning to taste with salt and pepper.

To make the ravioli: In the bowl of a food processor, combine the flour, 5 egg yolks, olive oil, and salt. Pulse for 30 seconds, or until the mixture has the texture of wet sand. Turn the mixture out onto a work surface and knead it with the palms of your hands to form a dough. Continue kneading for 2 to 3 minutes, until it is smooth and pliable. If you plan to roll out the dough by hand, rather than in a pasta machine, knead for several minutes longer. If the mixture is too dry to gather up into a ball after a minute or two of kneading, mix in an additional egg yolk. Gather the dough loosely into a ball, cover with plastic wrap, and let rest in the refrigerator for about 30 minutes.

If rolling by hand, use a wooden rolling pin on a clean, dry work surface. Roll out the dough as thinly as possible, forming a rectangular sheet roughly 12 x 14 inches. If using a pasta machine, roll the dough to the thinnest setting recommended by the manufacturer for making ravioli.

Cut the sheet in half, leaving both pieces on the work surface. Working down the edge of one sheet, place 1 tablespoon of the filling 1½ inches in from the side and top. Place another tablespoon of filling 3 inches below it. Repeat this step until you reach the bottom of the sheet. Make another vertical row of filling 3 inches from the first row. (If you are using pasta sheets rolled in a pasta machine, you may only be able to fit one row of ravioli on each sheet.) Repeat this step until you have used all the fillings to create eight evenly spaced portions of each filling, covering half of the total pasta sheets.

Lightly brush water around the mounds of filling. Gently lift the remaining pasta by loosely folding it, and unfold it over the sheet with the mounds of filling. Press down to seal the layers of pasta around the filling.

Using a 3-inch fluted cutter, cut round ravioli, making sure the edges are fully sealed. The ravioli can be made a day in advance kept, tightly covered with plastic wrap, in the refrigerator. They may also be frozen on a baking sheet, transferred to an airtight container or zipper-lock bag, and frozen for up to six weeks. Just before serving, bring a large pot of salted water to a boil. Gently slide the ravioli into the water and reduce the heat to medium, keeping the water at a very low boil for 3 minutes. If using frozen ravioli, do not thaw them before cooking, but add an extra minute to the cooking time. Gently remove the ravioli from the hot water and serve immediately with the Truffle Cream Sauce.

TRUFFLE CREAM SAUCE

*Truffle oil infuses this champagne cream sauce with a rich, full, irresistible flavor.
The sauce is also delicious served with fettuccine or penne. We usually make
our own truffle oil by steeping the peelings of white or black truffles in olive oil. When
buying truffle oil at a gourmet store, look for a good-quality white truffle oil
with no artificial flavoring. Some of the best truffle oils come from Italy.*

Makes 1½ cups

1 tablespoon unsalted butter

1 shallot, finely chopped (about 1½ tablespoons)

1 clove garlic, finely chopped

1 cup Vegetable Stock (see recipe on page 223)

1 cup heavy cream

1 cup champagne

Salt and freshly ground pepper, to taste

1 pound fresh baby spinach, picked over and washed

1 teaspoon truffle oil

¼ ounce fresh black truffle, very thinly sliced (optional)

Melt the butter in a medium sauté pan over low heat. Add the shallot and garlic and sauté for 3 minutes, until transparent but not browned. Add the Vegetable Stock, increase the heat to high, and cook until the liquid is reduced by half. Add the cream and ½ cup of champagne. Reduce over medium heat until the sauce has thickened enough to coat the back of a spoon. Season to taste with salt and pepper and strain through a fine sieve.

Bring two large pots of salted water to a boil. Add the spinach to one pot and cook for 2 minutes, until bright green and tender. Drain well. Add the ravioli to the other pot and cook as directed above for 3 minutes. Drain well.

While the spinach and ravioli are cooking, reheat the sauce, add the remaining ½ cup of champagne and the truffle oil, and stir to combine.

To serve, divide the spinach among four plates, placing it in the center of each plate. Gently slide the cooked ravioli into the sauce, then divide the ravioli among the plates. Drizzle the remaining sauce over the ravioli and spinach and serve immediately, topping with the truffle slices, if using.

EVERY NIGHT BEFORE DINNER,
THE SERVICE STAFF GATHERS FOR A PRE-MEAL
MEETING TO DISCUSS THE SPECIAL
NEEDS OF ANY GUESTS AND TO PLAN AHEAD
FOR THE SEAMLESS PRESENTATION
OF A COMPLEX MEAL.

Steamed Maine Lobster Nestled on a Bed of Homemade Fettuccine with Carrot, Ginger, Snow Peas, and a Cognac Coral Butter Sauce

This beautifully composed dish is one of the chef's signature presentations and a year-round favorite at the White Barn Inn. The steamed lobster is carefully shelled to keep the claw and tail meat intact. These are rearranged in the shape of a lobster atop a bed of lightly sauced fettucine, giving diners the pleasure of eating an entire lobster without the work of shelling it themselves.

Serves 4

4 (1½ pound) lobsters

½ cup heavy cream

1 cup Lobster Stock (see recipe on page 78)

½ cup cognac

2 sticks (½ pound) plus 2 tablespoons
unsalted butter, chilled

Salt and freshly ground pepper, to taste

1 (1-inch) piece ginger root, peeled

2 medium carrots, peeled

1 cup snow peas

1 pound fresh fettuccine

1 tablespoon extra-virgin olive oil

Bring a large stockpot filled with water to a boil. Plunge the lobsters headfirst into the water, submerging them completely, and boil for 9 minutes. Remove the lobsters from the boiling water and refresh in a bath of salted ice water. Break off the head cavity of each lobster, removing and reserving any coral or roe. Clean out the head, discarding the contents. Using kitchen shears, remove the lower part of the head shell, reserving the top of the shell with the antennae intact for garnish. Remove the tail and shell the claws, keeping the flesh whole, if possible. Using kitchen shears, cut off the bottom part of the tail shells and reserve for garnish.

In a large, heavy skillet, combine the cream, Lobster Stock, and cognac. Cook at a low boil over medium heat until reduced by half. Dice two sticks ($^{1}/_{2}$ pound) of the chilled butter and whisk into the sauce, along with the reserved lobster coral. Strain the sauce through a fine sieve into a medium saucepan, season to taste with salt and pepper, and keep warm over very low heat.

Cut the ginger, carrots, and snow peas into fine julienne, keeping each vegetable separate.

Place the ginger in a small saucepan of cold water and bring to a boil. Drain and repeat this process two more times, using fresh, cold water.

Fill a large stockpot and a large saucepan with salted water and bring to a boil. Add the fettuccine to the stockpot and cook for 5 minutes, or until tender but still firm. Drain and toss with the olive oil. Add the carrots to the saucepan of boiling water and cook for 2 minutes. Add the snow peas and continue cooking for 1 minute more. Drain and toss the vegetables with the remaining 2 tablespoons of butter, seasoning to taste with salt and pepper. Combine the fettuccine and vegetables in a large bowl and toss very gently to mix. Arrange in nests on the center of four dinner plates.

Gently reheat the lobster meat in the lobster coral sauce. Arrange the tail and claw meat in the shape of a whole lobster on top of each pasta nest, using the head and tail shells for garnish. Spoon the remaining sauce over the plates and serve immediately.

POIRE WILLIAM CRÈME BRÛLÉE ON A SABLÉ BISCUIT AND PEAR SORBET WITH SPICED PORT WINE SAUCE

*This elegant, layered dessert combines the warm, creamy texture
of crème brûlée with the cool, ever-so-slightly granular consistency of pear sorbet.
A crisp, sweet biscuit separates the two layers and adds yet another dimension of flavor and
texture. Each element of the dessert—the Poire William-infused crème brûlée
the pear sorbet, and the poached pears—brings out a subtly different aspect
of the fruit's flavor. Because the crème brûlée must be refrigerated overnight and the sorbet
needs to freeze for at least four hours before serving, this recipe is best started the day
before you plan to serve it. For a simpler dessert, prepare just the crème brûlée
or the sorbet, and serve with a garnish of poached pears.*

POIRE WILLIAM CRÈME BRÛLÉE

Serves 8

4 cups (1 quart) heavy cream

1½ cups milk

3 tablespoons Poire William, or other clear pear brandy

1½ cups egg yolks (15 to 18 yolks from large eggs)

1⅓ cups sugar, plus extra for the brûlée topping

2 eggs

8 Sablé Biscuits (see page 187)

Pear Sorbet (see page 188)

Poached Pears (see page 256)

Spiced Port Wine Sauce (see page 189)

Preheat the oven to 300°F.

In a medium saucepan with a heavy bottom, combine the cream, milk, and Poire William. Bring to a boil over medium heat.

In a large bowl, combine the egg yolks, whole eggs, and sugar. Using an electric mixer or whisking by hand, beat at medium speed for 5 minutes, until the mixture turns pale yellow.

Whisking constantly, add a quarter of the hot cream mixture to the egg mixture. When fully combined, gradually add the remaining cream mixture to the egg mixture, whisking continuously. Strain through a sieve to remove any lumps.

Pour the mixture into a 12 x 6-inch glass baking dish. Cover with aluminum foil. Place this dish inside a larger, deeper baking dish and add water to come halfway up the outside of the glass baking dish. Place in the center of the oven and bake for 1 hour to 1 hour and 15 minutes, until the custard becomes firm at the edges but still trembles slightly in the center. Remove from the oven, let cool to room temperature, and place in the refrigerator until it is fully chilled. Cover with plastic wrap and refrigerate overnight.

Just before serving, prepare a kitchen torch or preheat the oven to broil.

Arrange the Sablé Biscuits on an ungreased baking sheet. Using a 3-inch round cutter, cut disks of the chilled custard and place one on top of each biscuit. Sprinkle a light, even coating of sugar on top of each custard. Caramelize the sugar with a kitchen torch or place the baking sheet under a broiler, 3 to 5 inches below the heat source, until the sugar browns. Watch carefully to avoid burning. Arrange each serving of biscuit and crème brûlée on top of a disk of Pear Sorbet. Place in the center of a dessert plate, surround with the slices of Poached Pear, and drizzle with Spiced Port Wine Sauce.

SABLÉ BISCUITS

*Sablé is a French culinary term for sweet dough.
In this recipe, it yields a sweet, crisp biscuit that provides
the perfect layer between the cold sorbet and the just-browned
Crème Brûlée. This recipe is made with plenty of butter and
a light flour suitable for pastries or cakes.*

Makes 12 biscuits

1¾ sticks unsalted butter

¾ cup confectioners' sugar

2 egg yolks

1⅔ cups pastry or cake flour, sifted

Preheat oven to 350°F. Butter a baking sheet.

Place the butter and sugar in the bowl of a standing mixer. On medium speed, cream the mixture for about 5 minutes, until white and fluffy. Add the egg yolks and mix thoroughly. Add the sifted flour and mix by hand, stopping as soon as it is fully incorporated; take care not to overmix. Wrap the dough in plastic wrap and place in the refrigerator for 15 minutes.

Using a floured rolling pin, roll out the dough ¼ inch thick on a lightly floured cool surface, such as marble. Using a 3-inch cookie cutter, cut the dough into rounds, and arrange them 1 inch apart on a greased baking sheet. Bake for 8 to 10 minutes, until the cookies turn golden brown around the edges. Cool on a wire rack. These cookies are best served the day they are made, but they can be stored in an airtight container for one to two days, if necessary.

Pear Sorbet

*At the White Barn Inn, we make this sorbet with pear purée
purchased from a gourmet purveyor. To make your own purée, peel and core
three pears. Quarter the pears and place in a glass baking dish.
Cover with foil and bake in a 350°F oven for 20 minutes, until tender
but not browned. Purée until smooth in a food processor.*

Serves 8

2 cups pear purée

¾ cup sugar

Place the pear purée in a large, heatproof bowl. Combine the sugar with ½ cup of water in a medium saucepan and bring to a boil over medium high heat, stirring until the sugar is completely dissolved. Remove from heat and pour over the purée. If you are using homemade pear purée, allow the syrup to cool before adding to the purée. Let the mixture cool to room temperature, then cover and refrigerate.

Freeze the mixture in an ice cream machine, following the manufacturer's directions. Transfer the sorbet to a 12 x 6-inch glass dish, spreading it evenly, and place in the freezer for at least 4 hours, until firm. To serve with the Crème Brûlée above, cut the sorbet into 3-inch disks using a cookie cutter. Otherwise, serve small scoops of the sorbet as an intermediate course or a dessert. It keeps for up to two weeks in a covered container in the freezer.

SPICED PORT WINE SAUCE

Makes 1 cup

1 cup port

1 cup sugar

1 (6-inch) stick cinnamon

1 piece star anise

Pinch freshly ground white pepper

Pinch ground allspice

In a medium saucepan, combine 1 cup of water with the port, sugar, cinnamon, star anise, white pepper, and allspice. Bring to a boil over high heat. Reduce the heat to medium low and simmer for 15 to 20 minutes, until the sauce is reduced by half and has thickened enough to coat the back of a spoon. Remove from the heat and let cool. The sauce will thicken further upon cooling. The sauce can be kept in the refrigerator in an airtight container for three to four days.

OFFERING 8,000 BOTTLES FROM EVERY MAJOR WINE PRODUCING REGION IN THE WORLD, THE WINE CELLAR AT THE WHITE BARN INN INCLUDES THE PERFECT VINTAGE TO COMPLEMENT EVERY DISH. WITH A TUSCAN VINEYARD MURAL BY WELL-KNOWN LOCAL ARTIST JUDITH HARDENBROOK, THE WINE CELLAR SEATS UP TO 15 FOR PRIVATE PARTIES.

Romantic Fireside Dinner

The salad and entrée for this meal are relatively simple to prepare—perfect for a relaxed dinner with friends or a romantic evening at home. While the s'mores will require advance planning if you make the graham crackers and marshmallows from scratch, they are sure to delight everyone.

WARM FALL MUSHROOM SALAD WITH SHERRY VINAIGRETTE

Lightly sautéed and dressed with a slightly sweet sherry vinaigrette,
fall mushrooms lend a deliciously earthy flavor to this salad. At the White Barn Inn,
an expert forager provides us with an ever-changing supply of seasonal mushrooms.
Fall offerings include hen-of-the-woods, matsutake, black chanterelles, and
cèpes. If you don't have access to wild mushrooms, a mixture of cultivated mushrooms
such as porcini, cremini, oyster, or portobello makes a good substitute.

Serves 4

4 cups mesclun mix or
other mixed greens

1 cup mixed wild mushrooms,
lightly washed, drained, and towel dried

¼ cup sherry vinegar

½ cup extra-virgin olive oil

1 tablespoon blended oil (see Note)

Salt and freshly ground pepper

1 tablespoon diced shallot

2 tablespoons chopped chives

Wash and dry the mesclun and refrigerate until ready to serve. Trim the stems from the mushrooms and cut the mushrooms into bite-size pieces.

Measure the sherry vinegar into a small bowl and gradually whisk in the olive oil. Season to taste with salt and pepper.

In a medium skillet, warm the blended oil over medium heat. Add the shallots and sauté for a few seconds. Add the mushrooms and sauté, turning gently, for 2 to 3 minutes, until the mushrooms are soft. Add 2 tablespoons of the sherry dressing, season to taste with salt and pepper, and remove from the heat. Allow the mushrooms to cool for 3 to 5 minutes.

In a large bowl, combine the mesclun, mushrooms, and chopped chives. Add just enough dressing to coat the salad lightly, toss gently, and taste for seasoning. Divide the salad among four plates and serve immediately.

Note: Blended oil is a mixture of 90 percent vegetable oil and 10 percent olive oil.

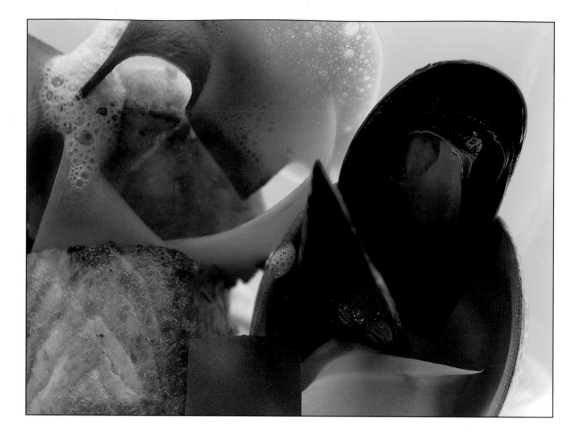

Ragout of Maine Salmon with Local Shellfish Medley and Saffron Champagne Sauce

*This elegant seafood mélange delights the eyes and the tongue.
Served in the shell, the clams and mussels have great visual appeal. Saffron lends
a golden tone to the sauce, and the colorful ribbons of lightly sautéed vegetables
are evocative of seaweed. If desired, accompany this dish with rice pilaf or boiled
potatoes tossed with plenty of butter and chopped dill or parsley.*

Serves 4

1 cup fruity white wine, such as Riesling

16 mahogany clams or other medium clams in the shell, scrubbed

16 mussels in the shell, scrubbed and debearded if necessary

2 tablespoons unsalted butter

1 shallot, diced

1 clove garlic, minced

Pinch saffron (about 20 threads)

1 cup heavy cream

1 cup champagne

Salt and freshly ground pepper

1 large celery root, peeled

1 large carrot, peeled

1 large Yukon Gold potato, peeled

1 large beet, peeled

1 pound skinless salmon filet, cut into 1-inch cubes

8 diver-harvested scallops

In a large skillet with a heavy bottom, bring the wine to a boil over medium high heat. Add the clams and mussels and cover. Cook, shaking the pan occasionally, until the shells open. Discard any clams or mussels with unopened shells. Strain the pan juices through a fine sieve lined with cheesecloth to remove any sand, and reserve.

Heat 1 tablespoon butter in a medium skillet over low heat and add the shallots, garlic, and saffron. Sauté for 3 minutes, until the shallots are translucent but not browned. Add 1 cup of the reserved pan juices, increase the heat to high, and boil, uncovered, until the mixture is reduced by half. Add the cream and ½ cup of champagne. Reduce the heat to medium and simmer until the sauce thickens enough to coat the back of a spoon. Add salt and pepper to taste and strain through a fine sieve.

Using a mandoline or an Asian vegetable slicer, cut the celery root, carrot, potato, and beet into ribbons 1 inch wide. Heat the remaining butter in a medium sauté pan over medium heat. Add the celery root, carrot, and potato, and cook, turning gently, for 1 or 2 minutes, just until tender. Add the beet ribbons and cook turning gently, for 1 to 2 minutes, just until tender. Remove from the heat.

Season the salmon and scallops with salt and pepper. In a deep skillet or casserole set over medium heat, combine the salmon and scallops with the remaining ½ cup of champagne. Bring to a boil, then reduce the heat to medium and cook for 2 to 3 minutes, just until the salmon and scallops are tender, with rare centers.

Add the cooked mussels and clams, reserved sauce, and vegetable ribbons to the skillet, stirring gently to combine without breaking up the salmon. Serve immediately in large, warmed soup bowls.

S'MORES

*Growing up in England, I had never encountered s'mores until I came
to America. Toasting these sweet little sandwiches by the fire is the perfect way
to take the nip out of a cold day. If you make the graham crackers and
marshmallows from scratch, you can transform this simple campfire recipe
into a gourmet treat to enjoy on a romantic fireside evening.*

Makes 12

24 Cinnamon Graham Crackers (see page 195)

12 good-quality milk chocolate bars (1 ounce each)

12 Marshmallows (see page 196)

Arrange the Cinnamon Graham Crackers on a large platter. Place one chocolate bar on twelve of the graham crackers.

Using a long-handled barbecue fork, toast each marshmallow over an open fire until golden brown. Immediately place a toasted marshmallow on a chocolate-topped graham cracker. Cover with another cracker and press gently to make a sandwich.

Let stand for 1 minute to soften the chocolate, then eat while warm. Repeat with the remaining ingredients.

WHILE THE KITCHEN STAFF PREPARES THE ELEMENTS
OF EACH EVENING'S DINNER, THE SERVICE STAFF ATTENDS TO
ALL THE DETAILS OF AN ELEGANT TABLE INCLUDING
CRISPLY PRESSED LINENS AND WELL-POLISHED TABLEWARE.

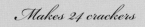

Makes 24 crackers

2 cups whole wheat flour

1 cup all-purpose flour

1 teaspoon baking powder

½ teaspoon baking soda

Pinch salt

¾ cup brown sugar, packed

½ cup vegetable shortening

⅓ cup honey

1 teaspoon vanilla extract

½ cup milk

3 tablespoons sugar

1 teaspoon ground cinnamon

In a large bowl, whisk together the flours, baking powder, baking soda, and salt. In another large bowl, combine the brown sugar with the shortening, and cream until smooth. Using an electric mixer or a wooden spoon, beat in the honey and vanilla until light and fluffy.

Add the dry ingredients to the shortening mixture, alternating with the milk mixture. Beat well after each addition until the ingredients are fully incorporated.

Wrap the dough in plastic wrap and refrigerate for several hours or overnight. Preheat the oven to 350°F.

Divide the chilled dough into quarters. On a well-floured surface, roll each quarter into a 15 x 5-inch rectangle. Cut each rectangle into six small rectangles measuring 5 x 2½ inches each. Place the rectangles on an ungreased baking sheet. Make a line across the center of each rectangle with the tines of fork and score a regular pattern of holes on each cracker. You can also score initials or decorative patterns.

In a small bowl, combine the sugar and cinnamon. Sprinkle the mixture evenly over the crackers. Bake the crackers for 13 to 15 minutes, until golden-brown at the edges and firm to the touch. Remove from the baking sheet at once and cool on a wire rack.

MARSHMALLOWS

*These homemade marshmallows can be prepared a week in advance
and stored in an airtight container in the refrigerator.*

Makes 12 marshmallows

2 cups sugar

2 tablespoons powdered gelatin
soaked in ½ cup cold water

1 teaspoon vanilla extract

¼ teaspoon salt

2 tablespoons confectioners' sugar,
plus additional for dusting

2 tablespoons cornstarch

In a medium saucepan with a heavy bottom, combine the granulated sugar
and ¾ cup water. Bring to a boil and cook to the soft-ball stage (238°F on a
candy thermometer). Soft-ball stage is achieved when a small amount of
syrup dropped into a cup of cold water forms a soft ball that flattens out but
does not fall apart when picked up with a spoon. Remove from the heat and
stir in the dissolved gelatin.

Transfer the mixture to a glass bowl and let cool to room temperature.
Using an electric mixer, whip the mixture until thick and white. Stir in the
vanilla extract, salt, confectioners' sugar, and cornstarch.

Spread the mixture evenly into a 9-inch square pan. Cool, uncovered, in
the refrigerator until firm. Using a wet knife to prevent sticking, cut into
twelve squares. Dust lightly with confectioners' sugar and enjoy.

MULLED APPLE CIDER

*There's nothing like a hot mug of mulled cider or Irish coffee
to warm up a cold evening. This recipe, infused with spices and orange peel,
is delicious with or without the addition of rum.*

Serves 2

2 cups fresh apple cider

1 (6-inch) cinnamon stick

⅛ teaspoon ground nutmeg

Peel of 1 medium orange

2 ounces dark rum or spiced rum (optional)

In a medium saucepan, combine the cider, cinnamon, nutmeg, and orange peel and
bring to a boil over medium heat. Remove the pan from the heat and allow the mixture
to infuse for 20 minutes. Strain through a medium sieve into a clean saucepan. Heat
over medium heat until hot. Add the rum, if using, and divide between two glass mugs.

CONSTANT COMMUNICATION
BETWEEN THE KITCHEN STAFF AND THE SERVICE STAFF
ENSURES THAT EVERY DETAIL IS ADDRESSED, AND
THAT EACH COURSE IS PRESENTED WITH PRECISE ATTENTION
TO TIMING, TEMPERATURE, AND APPEARANCE.

IRISH COFFEE

*At the White Barn Inn, we serve our Irish coffee with
a generous amount of whiskey. If you prefer a less alcoholic drink,
try adding just one ounce of whiskey instead of two.*

Serves 2

4 ounces Jameson Irish whiskey

2 cups hot, freshly brewed coffee

6 teaspoons whipped cream (lightly sweetened, if desired)

Cocoa powder

Warm two heat-resistant glass cups with hot water. Pour out the hot water and divide the whiskey between the cups. Fill with hot coffee and top with whipped cream. Sprinkle with cocoa powder and serve immediately.

Autumn Ingredients

WILD MUSHROOMS

Hen-of-the-woods, also called maitake, are large, ridged mushrooms that grow beneath maples and oaks and flourish in the cool fall weather. The even larger cauliflower mushrooms (mature ones can measure 6 to 8 inches in width) spring up beneath trees that are dropping their leaves. Colorful cèpes with tall caps nestle among the roots of blue spruce trees, and the white matsutake grow only on sleep slopes under hemlock trees.

CRANBERRIES

These bright berries are synonymous with autumn in New England. One of the few fruits native to North America (along with blueberries and Concord grapes), they thrive in low temperatures and can be harvested from cranberry bogs as late as November. Their tart taste, balanced with a judicious amount of sugar, creates a delicious accompaniment to the season's earthy, savory flavors.

PEARS

Pears are an abundant early autumn fruit that make wonderful additions to seasonal tossed green salads. They come in many sizes, shapes, and textures, from tiny, firm Seckel pears to the larger, softer-fleshed Comice pears. Roasted pears make flavorful garnishes for meat entrees, and pear purée forms the basis for a delicious fall sorbet.

APPLES

Many varieties of apples are harvested in Maine's orchards from late August through October, including McIntosh, Cortland, Macoun, and Northern Spy. Apples add sweetness and fall flavor, whether sliced raw into salads, simmered in a ragout of root vegetables, or sautéed with sugar for dessert.

LOBSTER

Lobsters grow by molting their shells, shedding every year up to the age of seven. They grow their new shells during the warmer summer months. By the time the ocean cools down in the fall, lobsters have formed new shells and their flesh becomes firm and particularly succulent. The chef at The White Barn Inn considers autumn the best time for eating the crustaceans, whether steaming them and enjoying them straight out of the shell with lemon butter or pairing the sweet meat with delicately flavored cream sauces.

PUMPKIN

The bright flesh of pumpkins is remarkably versatile. It may be blended with cream to make a mild-flavored soup with an extraordinary pale orange color, or with spices and eggs to form a zesty pie filling. The seeds of the pumpkin add a deliciously nutty flavor to salads, whether roasted and scattered on top as a garnish or infused into a richly flavored dressing made with pumpkinseed oil.

Winter at the
WHITE BARN INN

In Maine, winter is called the Silent Season, perhaps because so many of the state's seasonal residents, both avian and human, flock to warmer climates, leaving behind an eerily serene landscape. In early December Canadian geese soar in wavering formations across the sky, their haunting cries piercing the thin, cold air. Great nor'easters sweep in, bringing powerful winds that buffet the sea and shore, and clouds of snow that swirl in white-on-white frenzy. Days of exquisite calm often follow, when a crescent moon hangs like a sliver of ice in the afternoon sky and a faint pink glow along the western horizon presages early sunset.

Kennebunkport's year-round residents and a devoted population of off-season visitors cherish winter's particular pleasures. Wrapped in sweaters and hats, they take dogs for long romps on Mother's Beach, where the surf freezes along the water's edge and frozen sea foam skitters across the sand. Or they strike out for exhilarating walks along Ocean Avenue, savoring the crystalline light that accentuates the colors and textures of the ever-changing seascape. At Spouting Rock, deep blue and luminous green waves explode with arcs of spray against snow-limned ledges of black and purple stone. Along the marshes lining the Kennebunk River, snow clings to the windblown plants, its pale dust contrasting against golden blades of marsh grass, the soft brown rods of cattails, and clusters of crimson berries.

Although most of the pleasure craft are stowed for the season, lobster boats still ply the icy waters, their brightly painted hulls and droning motors venturing out at dawn while most sleepers still snuggle deeply into down-lined beds. Other fishermen gather succulent fruits of the winter sea, including Maine oysters, mussels, and North Atlantic shrimp caught several hundred miles offshore. Deep in the woods, hunters claim deer and pheasant that will be savored at the Christmas table alongside the season's hearty vegetables: sweet potatoes, celery root, turnips, and cabbage, both red and green.

These ingredients shine in sophisticated presentations at the White Barn Inn during Christmas Prelude, a weeklong celebration in early December when the entire town of Kennebunkport heralds the beginning of

Inn to celebrate Christmas, ring in the New Year, or indulge in a Valentine's Day escape-for-two.

Throughout the holiday season, chef Jonathan Cartwright revels in the delights of the winter table, ranging from the decadent excess of Christmas and New Year's Eve feasts replete with oysters, foie gras, and wine-rich sauces to the simple pleasure of a bowl of hearty soup. Since winter is a time when family and

. . . the White Barn Inn during Christmas Prelude, a weeklong celebration in early December when the entire town of Kennebunkport heralds the beginning of the holidays. Miles of evergreen garland decorate sidewalks and doorways, and at night, glittering strands of light illumine the homes and shops.

the holidays. Miles of evergreen garland decorate sidewalks and doorways, and at night, glittering strands of light illumine the homes and shops. On the first Friday of the Prelude, guests gather at the Inn for a festive cocktail party, where champagne flows and caviar-topped canapés of oysters and salmon tartare are nibbled from silver spoons. The following evening they join the townspeople for roasted chestnuts and Christmas carols on the grounds of the local Franciscan monastery. Many guests return year after year to the

friends enjoy meeting over food and drinks, the chef also suggests two party menus, for a holiday cocktail gathering and a New Year's Day brunch, that promise to dazzle guests. Together, these recipes and entertaining ideas reveal the full spectrum of winter's joys, from the sociable feast to the quietly romantic stroll in the snow. The chef recommends a bracing walk by the sea as the perfect antidote to holiday feasting, with a pocketful of warm, freshly roasted chestnuts and a thermal flask of spiced wine or rum-spiked tea.

WINTER MENUS

Winter by the Sea

Spiced Nuts

Grissini Breadsticks

Roasted Chestnuts

Christmas Present Hunters' Tea

Glühwein

Velvety Pheasant and Chestnut Soup

•

Christmas Prelude Dinner at the White Barn Inn

Kennebunkport Lobster on Mango Salsa
with Golden Osetra Caviar and Lobster Mayonnaise

Truffled Celeriac Soup

Pan Seared New England Venison Cutlet
with a Caramelized Sweet Potato Timbale, Red Cabbage,
and Elderberry Sauce

or

Tenderloin of Beef Glazed in a Foie Gras Crust
on a Potato Rösti with Madeira Sauce

Warm Chocolate Cake with Warm Chocolate Sauce
and Vanilla Bean Ice Cream

A Holiday Cocktail Party

Northern Lights Cocktail

Maine Oyster Canapés

Pan-seared North Atlantic Shrimp
and Quail Egg Canapés

Duck Confit and Apple Pasties

Feta Cheese and Spinach Rolls

Maine Peekie Toe Crab Cakes

Marinated Salmon Tartar with Golden Osetra Caviar

•

A New Year's Day Brunch

Cold-Smoked Maine Salmon with
Creamy Scrambled Eggs

Apple French Toast

Pineapple Coconut Granola

Ham and Mozzarella Quiche

Poached Pears

Prunes Poached with Cinnamon and Port

Winter by the Sea

It's tempting to stay indoors when the weather turns cold, but a walk along the water's edge at sunset can be the perfect antidote to winter's ennui or holiday overindulgence. By planning ahead and filling your pockets with a bag of roasted nuts and a thermal flask with a hot drink, you can transform a chilly walk into a delightful outing. When you return, there is no better way to reward a well-honed appetite than with a hot bowl of soup and just-baked breadsticks.

SPICED NUTS

This delicious snack combines the textures
of pecans, cashews, almonds, and pumpkin seeds with a
spice mix of dried red chiles, black pepper, and
yellow curry powder. Diners at the White Barn Inn enjoy
these nuts served warm at the bar with cocktails.
They can be prepared in minutes and make a healthy snack
to munch on a wintertime walk, as well as
a perfect cocktail nibble for dinner
parties at home.

Makes 1¾ cups

½ cup shelled pecans

½ cup unsalted cashews

½ cup unsalted almonds

4 tablespoons pumpkin seeds

1 tablespoon olive oil

⅛ teaspoon cayenne pepper

¹/₈ teaspoon chili powder

¹/₄ teaspoon curry powder

¹/₄ teaspoon salt

¹/₄ teaspoon freshly ground black pepper

Preheat the oven to 450°F.

In a large bowl, combine all of the ingredients. Toss until the nuts and seeds are completely coated with the spice mixture. Taste for seasoning and add more cayenne, chili, and curry powder if you prefer a spicier taste. Transfer the nuts to a baking sheet and bake for 1 to 2 minutes, just until the nuts begin to sizzle and the seeds begin to pop. Watch carefully to avoid burning the nuts. Serve warm, or cool on the baking sheet and transfer to an airtight container. Nuts will keep at room temperature in a sealed container for two weeks.

GRISSINI BREADSTICKS

*These crisp, thin breadsticks make a delicious accompaniment to salads and
soups or a great cocktail snack that won't spoil guests' appetites. They are a favorite at
Grissini, the White Barn Inn's sister restaurant in nearby Kennebunk, which takes
its name from the Italian word for breadsticks. There, they are baked in a wood-fired
oven alongside pizza, grilled steak, seafood, and fowl. But they may be prepared
just as effectively in a conventional oven at home and are a simple bread to master.*

Makes 30 12-inch breadsticks

2½ cups sifted bread flour

1 cup semolina flour

2 teaspoons (½ ounce) dry yeast

2 teaspoons salt

1½ tablespoons olive oil

Dried Italian herb mixture,
poppy or sesame seeds, or sea salt (optional)

In an electric mixer fitted with a dough hook, combine the flours, yeast, and salt.
Mixing at low speed, gradually add the oil and 1¼ cups water until the wet and dry
ingredients are fully combined and form a soft dough. Knead for a few minutes,
until smooth and pliable. Cover the dough with a dry towel and let it rest at room
temperature for 20 minutes.

Preheat the oven to 375°F.

Divide the dough into ten evenly sized balls. On a floured work surface, roll each
dough ball into a cylinder 36 inches in length. Cut each into three 12-inch sticks.
Arrange 1 inch apart on an ungreased baking sheet. If desired, sprinkle lightly with
dried Italian herb mixture, poppy or sesame seeds, or sea salt. Bake for 40 minutes,
until golden brown and crisp. Cool slightly on the baking sheet and serve warm.
Breadsticks are best eaten the day they are made but can be stored in an airtight container for 3 days.

ROASTED CHESTNUTS

*In England and New England, chestnuts roasting by an open fire
have been a quintessential part of Christmas for centuries. At the White Barn Inn,
where 200 pounds of chestnuts are roasted and served to carolers during
the Christmas Prelude each year, they are true harbingers of the holiday season.
Throughout most of the country, raw chestnuts are available in the produce
section of quality grocery stores. They are simple to prepare, and you will find
the sweetly nutty aroma they exude during roasting irresistible.*

Makes 2 pounds

2 pounds fresh chestnuts

Preheat a charcoal grill. Using the tip of a sharp knife, pierce a cross on the pointed tip of each chestnut, opposite the dark flat circle on the nut's base. Once all the flames have subsided, arrange the chestnuts in a single layer on the grill over the glowing coals. If the bars of the grill are spaced too widely, use a grilling basket to keep the nuts from falling into the fire. Alternately, chestnuts can be roasted in a metal basket or on a grate placed near the embers of an open fireplace. Cook the chestnuts for 10 to 12 minutes, turning frequently, until the cut edges of the shell curl slightly and the chestnut meat is tender but still moist.

Christmas Present Hunters' Tea

*European hunters have long enjoyed hot tea fortified with alcohol
during or after a day spent stalking game in cold fields and forests. This version of
hunters' tea, spiked with mint-flavored schnapps and rum, is guaranteed
to soothe the winter shivers, whether brought on by a day of hunting or an afternoon
of holiday shopping. When serving this tea to guests, the ceremony of igniting
the rum-soaked sugar cubes adds a festive and memorable touch to the presentation.*

Serves 4

4 slices lemon

8 sugar cubes

4 cups freshly brewed black tea, such as Darjeeling

2 teaspoons peppermint schnapps

4 teaspoons white rum

Place one slice of lemon and one sugar cube in each of four heat-resistant glass cups. Divide the hot tea evenly among the cups. Add ½ teaspoon of peppermint schnapps to each cup. Place the remaining sugar cubes on four teaspoons arranged on a heat-proof plate. Pour 1 teaspoon of rum over each sugar cube. Set the sugar cubes on fire and add the burning cubes to the tea.

GLÜHWEIN

*Glühwein (glue-vine), a citrus-and-spice-mulled red wine, is a
traditional German winter beverage. It is best prepared with Cabernet Sauvignon
or Merlot, but even an inexpensive table wine makes a tasty cup of glühwein.
Some people prefer it mulled with orange peel and juice instead of
lemon, and others add more alcohol, such as spiced rum or flavored schnapps.
Experiment with this throughout the winter months to create
your own favorite version.*

Serves 4

4 cups full-bodied red wine,
such as Merlot or Cabernet Sauvignon

1 cup sugar

1 (3-inch) stick cinnamon

2 whole cloves

½ lemon, peeled and juiced

In a large saucepan over medium high heat, combine all of the ingredients and bring
to a boil. Remove from the heat and serve immediately in heat-resistant glass cups,
or store in a thermal container until ready to drink.

GLEAMING DECANTERS OF BRANDY
AND A FULL AFTERNOON TEA SERVICE COMPLETE WITH
FINGER SANDWICHES AND SCONES GREET GUESTS
EACH AFTERNOON. THESE REFRESHMENTS CAN BE ENJOYED
IN THE BREAKFAST ROOM OR SAVORED BESIDE
A FIRE IN THE COOLER MONTHS.

VELVETY PHEASANT AND CHESTNUT SOUP

*Chestnuts make an exceptionally rich soup when puréed with flavorful stock
and cream. This recipe combines savory, slow-cooked stock made from
roasted pheasant with the sweet nuttiness of chestnuts. While the chopped pheasant
breast makes a lovely addition to the soup, it is optional, which makes this soup
a wonderful way to use the remains of a pheasant enjoyed for dinner the night
before (or even frozen from a previous meal). If you don't want to go
to the trouble of roasting and peeling chestnuts, you can use packaged,
precooked chestnuts, available in gourmet stores.*

Serves 4

1 Roast Pheasant, about 3 pounds before cooking (see page 214)

4 tablespoons (½ stick) unsalted butter

1 medium carrot, peeled and diced

1 medium onion, diced

2 celery stalks, diced

3 sprigs fresh rosemary

3 sprigs fresh thyme

2 cloves garlic

1 cup fruity white wine, such as Riesling

¾ pound (about 2½ cups) shelled, roasted chestnuts (see page 210)

1 cup heavy cream

Salt and freshly ground black pepper

Preheat the oven to 450°F.

Remove the breasts from the roasted pheasant and reserve. Place the pheasant carcass with legs attached in a large roasting pan. Roast, turning occasionally, for 15 minutes, until golden brown.

Melt the butter in a large stockpot over medium heat. Add the carrot, onion, celery, rosemary, thyme, and garlic and sauté until the vegetables are soft but not browned. Remove the pheasant from the oven and add it to the stockpot. Add the wine, plus enough water to cover the bones. Simmer over medium low heat for 6 hours, until the stock is dark golden brown and richly flavored. Strain through a fine sieve. You should have about 4 cups of stock.

In a blender or food processor, combine the stock with all but ½ cup of the shelled chestnuts. Purée the mixture for a few minutes until it is smooth.

Pour the soup into a clean saucepan and bring to a simmer over medium heat. Add the cream and season to taste with salt and pepper.

Cut the reserved pheasant breasts and reserved chestnuts into ½ inch dice. Serve the soup hot, garnished with diced pheasant breast and chestnuts.

ROAST PHEASANT

Serves 2 to 4

1 pheasant (about 3 pounds)

Salt and freshly ground pepper

1 clove garlic

1 small sprig fresh rosemary

1 small spring fresh thyme

2 tablespoons blended oil (see Note)

Preheat the oven to 350°F.

Season the pheasant inside and out with salt and pepper. Place the garlic, rosemary, and thyme in the cavity of the pheasant and rub the outside with the oil. Place on one side in a roasting pan and roast for five minutes. Turn the pheasant over and roast for five minutes more. Turn breast-side up and continue roasting for 45 minutes, until the pheasant is golden brown and the juices run clear when the breast is pierced with a fork. Allow to rest for ten minutes, then carve as desired.

Note: Blended oil is a mixture of 90 percent vegetable oil and 10 percent olive oil.

Christmas Prelude Dinner at the White Barn Inn

Guests at the White Barn Inn begin their holiday feasting early with the Christmas Prelude dinner, a five-course meal that combines many of the traditional delights of the winter table: sweet morsels of lobster, creamy soup, lean and flavorful game paired with robust vegetables, and a warm chocolate dessert. Gourmet touches such as a drizzle of truffle oil and the transformation of the lowly sweet potato into a custardy timbale add festive elegance to this menu.

KENNEBUNKPORT LOBSTER ON MANGO SALSA WITH GOLDEN OSETRA CAVIAR AND LOBSTER MAYONNAISE

This colorful dish can be served in bite-size portions that tease the tongue,
or in a larger serving that can replace the Truffled Celeriac Soup as a first course.
In addition to pleasing the eye with its beautiful shades of red and orange,
this dish explodes with a combination of sweet, tart, and salty flavors,
plus contrasting crisp and creamy textures.

Serves 4 as a first course or
8 as an amuse-bouche

2 (1¼-pound) lobsters

¼ cup Lobster Oil (see page 219)

1 ripe mango, peeled, seeded, and cut into ⅛-inch dice

1 red bell pepper, seeded and cut into ⅛-inch dice

1 shallot, finely diced

1 tablespoon chopped chives

1 tablespoon champagne vinegar

2 tablespoons blended oil (see Note)

Pinch cayenne pepper

1 lime

2 tablespoons sherry vinegar

1 large egg yolk

1 teaspoon Dijon mustard

Salt and freshly ground black pepper

$\frac{1}{4}$ ounce golden osetra caviar

Bring 2 large pots of salted water to a boil over high heat. Add one lobster, head first, to each pot. Cook at a boil for 8 minutes. Remove the pots from the heat and let the lobsters cool to room temperature in the cooking liquid. Drain and shell the lobsters, reserving the shell and any coral for the Lobster Oil. (Lobster coral, or roe, is the cluster of eggs found at the top of the tail of the female lobster. Uncooked coral is dark blue; once steamed, it takes on a reddish hue.) Although lobster tastes best on the day it is cooked, the shelled meat will keep tightly wrapped in plastic in the refrigerator for up to three days. For best flavor, bring it to room temperature before serving.

Prepare the Lobster Oil (see page 219).

In a medium nonreactive glass or stainless steel bowl, combine the mango, red bell pepper, shallot, and chives. Add the champagne vinegar and blended oil and season to taste with a pinch of cayenne pepper and the juice of $\frac{1}{2}$ lime.

In a medium nonreactive bowl, whisk together the sherry vinegar, egg yolk, and Dijon mustard. Gradually add the Lobster Oil, whisking continuously to form an emulsion.

Season the mayonnaise to taste with salt and pepper and, if desired, a pinch of cayenne pepper and a few drops of lime juice.

Divide the mango salsa evenly among the plates. Divide the lobster into equal portions consisting of tail, claw, and knuckle meat and arrange on top of the salsa. Garnish the lobster with caviar and drizzle the mayonnaise around the outside of the plate.

Note: Blended oil is a mixture of 90 percent vegetable oil and 10 percent olive oil.

LOBSTER OIL

This infused oil contributes the essence of lobster
to sauces and salad dressings. For more intense flavor,
try adding it to the mayonnaise used for Lobster Rolls (see page 106).
The lobster shells create a reddish-gold tint, making the oil
a colorful element in such recipes as the Lobster Spring Roll on page 59.
Lobster oil can be stored in an airtight container
in the refrigerator for 2 weeks.

1 pound lobster shells

1 teaspoon lobster coral (if available)

½ cup blended oil (see Note)

Preheat the oven to 300°F.

Clean out the head cavities of the shells, discarding the contents. Cut the shells into 1-inch pieces and place them on a baking sheet. Bake for 10 minutes to dry.

Reduce the oven temperature to 160°F. Transfer the dried shells to a wide, shallow, ovenproof pan. Add the coral and blended oil and toss to coat the shells with oil. Gently heat on the stove top over low heat until the oil is warm but not sizzling, then transfer the pan to the oven. Cook for at least 2 hours and no longer than 3 hours, stirring occasionally, to infuse the oil with the flavor of the lobster shells. When the oil has turned a rich golden red, strain it through a fine sieve, pressing on the shells to extract all the oil. Discard the solids, let the oil cool to room temperature, and refrigerate until ready to use.

Note: Blended oil is a mixture of 90 percent vegetable oil and 10 percent olive oil.

TRUFFLED CELERIAC SOUP

While sharing the mild flavor of the familiar celery stalk,
the root known as celeriac has the added benefit of a smooth, starchy texture
that can be transformed into delicious purées and creamy soups.
A touch of truffle oil enriches the flavor, adding an intense note that is at once
earthy and ethereal. The optional shavings of fresh truffle provide another
degree of elegance for this sensational winter soup.

Serves 8

2 tablespoons unsalted butter

1 tablespoon olive oil

½ medium onion, diced

2 pounds celery root (celeriac),
peeled and cut into 1-inch dice (2 large roots)

1 sprig fresh thyme

1 sprig fresh rosemary

1 cup dry white wine, such as chardonnay

1 cup Chicken Stock or Vegetable Stock (see page 222 or 223)

4 cups heavy cream

Salt and freshly ground black pepper

Truffle oil, to taste

1 black truffle, thinly sliced (optional)

In a large pot, melt the butter with the olive oil over medium heat. Add the onion and celery root and sauté for 3 minutes, until the onion begins to soften. Add the thyme and rosemary and sauté for 3 minutes. Cover, reduce the heat to low, and cook for 5 minutes, stirring occasionally. Add the wine and stock and bring the soup to a boil over medium heat. Add the cream and continue to boil for 2 minutes. Reduce the heat to low, cover, and simmer for 15 minutes, until the celery root is tender.

Working in batches, purée the soup in a blender or food processor until smooth. Strain it through a fine sieve into a clean pan. Season to taste with salt and pepper. Just before serving, return the soup to a boil to reheat it. Whisk in 1 tablespoon of truffle oil by hand or with a handheld blender. Taste the soup; if you prefer a stronger truffle flavor, add a little more truffle oil. Serve in individual soup bowls, garnished with slices of black truffle if desired.

CHAIRS CLAD IN GLOVE-SOFT ESPRESSO-COLORED ITALIAN LEATHER AWAIT DINNER GUESTS AT THE WHITE BARN INN. PEWTER CHARGERS AND FANCIFUL SCULPTURES MADE FROM SILVER CUTLERY BY FRENCH ARTIST GIRARD BOUVIER PROVIDE GLEAMING HIGHLIGHTS WITHIN THE RUSTIC SETTING OF THE CONVERTED COUNTRY BARN.

Chicken Stock

Makes 3 cups

4 pounds chicken bones

½ pound mixed aromatic vegetables,
such as carrots, leeks, onions, and celery, diced

1 clove garlic, crushed

12 sprigs fresh herbs,
such as thyme, rosemary, and tarragon

1 cup dry white wine, such as chardonnay

Preheat the oven to 450°F.

Place the bones in a large roasting pan and roast, turning occasionally, for 15 minutes, until golden brown. Add the vegetables to the pan and continue roasting for 5 minutes.

Transfer the bones and vegetables to a large stockpot and add the garlic, herbs, and white wine. Cover with water and bring to a boil over high heat, skimming off any scum that rises to the surface. Reduce the heat to medium and simmer for four hours, until reduced by half.

Strain the stock through a fine sieve. To use for sauces, simmer the strained stock over medium heat until it is reduced by half. Store in an airtight container in the refrigerator for up to three days or freeze in ice cube trays, then transfer the stock cubes to zipper-lock bags and freeze for up to 1 month.

Vegetable Stock

This versatile stock can be used as the base for many soups.
Feel free to vary the ingredients to reflect what is available in your
vegetable bin. Also, you may want to add more of the vegetable
that will be the primary flavor of the finished soup.

$\frac{1}{4}$ cup vegetable oil

1 medium butternut squash, peeled,
seeded, and chopped

2 celery stalks, chopped

1 leek, chopped

1 medium onion, peeled and chopped

1 medium carrot, peeled and chopped

4 medium tomatoes, chopped

1 sprig fresh thyme

1 sprig fresh parsley

1 clove garlic, chopped

1 cup dry white wine, such as chardonnay

5 whole peppercorns

Salt and freshly ground pepper

In a large stockpot, warm the oil over medium heat. Add the vegetables, herbs, and garlic and stir to coat with the oil. Cover and cook, stirring occasionally, for 5 minutes. Add the wine and 3 quarts of water and bring to a boil. Reduce the heat to medium low, add the peppercorns, and simmer for 2 hours. Strain through a fine sieve and season to taste with salt and pepper. Store in an airtight container in the refrigerator for up to three days or freeze in ice cube trays, transferring the cubes of stock to zipper-lock bags, and freeze for up to 1 month.

Pan Seared New England Venison Cutlet
with a Caramelized Sweet Potato Timbale,
Red Cabbage, and Elderberry Sauce

Thanks to the increased availability of farm-raised venison, this lean and flavorful
meat is now available year-round. But the traditional season for hunting—
and eating—game is winter. Relatively simple to prepare (especially if you
already have Veal Jus on hand or make one by diluting a high-quality commercially
prepared meat glaze), this beautiful main course is highly rewarding. For the sauce,
I like to use preserved elderberries, which are available at gourmet shops,
but preserved blueberries are equally delicious, and the sauce also
tastes great without any berries at all.

Serves 4

2 tablespoons red wine vinegar

2 tablespoons plus ¼ cup full-bodied red wine,
such as Merlot or Cabernet Sauvignon

1 tablespoon honey

Salt and freshly ground black pepper

½ head red cabbage, outer leaves and core discarded, thinly sliced

3 tablespoons unsalted butter

¼ cup diced onion

2 ounces (about ⅓ cup) lean trimmings from
beef, venison, or other red meat

1 sprig fresh thyme

1 teaspoon cracked black peppercorns

2 tablespoons port

2 cups Veal Jus (see page 68)

¼ cup preserved elderberries

1 cup brussels sprouts, outer leaves discarded, halved

4 venison rack chops or tenderloin filets (about 5 ounces each)

1 tablespoon blended oil (see Note)

4 Caramelized Sweet Potato Timbales (see page 227)

In a large nonreactive glass or stainless steel bowl, whisk together the vinegar, 2 tablespoons wine, and honey with salt and pepper to taste. Add the sliced cabbage and toss to combine. Cover with plastic wrap and marinate at room temperature for 12 hours.

Heat 1 tablespoon of butter in a medium saucepan over low heat. Add the diced onion and sauté for 3 to 4 minutes, until translucent but not browned. Add the venison trimmings and cook for 1 minute on high heat, until the trimmings are seared. Add the remaining ¼ cup wine, thyme, and cracked peppercorns. Bring to a boil, then reduce the heat to medium and simmer for 2 to 3 minutes. Add the port and the Veal Jus and return the sauce to a boil over high heat. Reduce the heat to medium and simmer for 5 to 8 minutes, until the sauce is glossy and has thickened enough to coat the back of a spoon. Strain the sauce through a fine sieve and season to taste with salt and pepper. Stir in the elderberries.

Bring a medium saucepan of salted water to a boil. Add the brussels sprouts and boil for 6 to 8 minutes, just until tender. Drain.

Season the venison with salt and pepper. Heat the blended oil in a large skillet over high heat. Add the venison and sear for 5 to 10 seconds. Add ½ tablespoon of butter to the pan and continue to cook over high heat for 3 to 5 minutes on each side for medium-rare venison. For medium venison, cook for 7 minutes on each side.

While the venison is cooking, melt 1 tablespoon of butter in a saucepan over medium heat. Add the brussels sprouts and reheat gently, tossing to coat them with the butter, and season to taste with salt and pepper.

Melt the remaining ½ tablespoon of butter in a large skillet over medium heat. Add the red cabbage and any marinating liquid and sauté for 2 to 3 minutes, until tender but still slightly crisp. Season to taste with salt and pepper.

To serve, place one Caramelized Sweet Potato Timbale and a mound of red cabbage on each plate. If using chops, make a cut in each chop from the bottom up to the bone. Open the meat up, seasoning the cut surface with salt and pepper, and place it on top of the cabbage. If using tenderloin, serve filets whole. Spoon the elderberry sauce over and around the venison. Arrange a spoonful of brussels sprouts on one side of the plate.

Note: Blended oil is a mixture of 90 percent vegetable oil and 10 percent olive oil.

CARAMELIZED SWEET POTATO TIMBALE

*The sweet potato is a colorful, tasty root vegetable that is often overlooked.
It gives these timbales a beautiful pale-orange color. Their well-rounded,
gently sweet flavor is heightened by the layer of caramelized sugar that makes
them taste like slightly savory portions of crème caramel. To prepare
in advance, store the caramelized timbales and sweet potato custard mixture
separately in the refrigerator for up to three days. Bring to room
temperature and bake as instructed below.*

Makes 8 timbales

1½ pounds sweet potatoes
(about 1 large or 2 small potatoes), peeled

¾ cup sugar

5 eggs

2 cups heavy cream

¼ teaspoon salt

Freshly ground black pepper

Nutmeg

Preheat the oven to 300°F.

Slice the sweet potatoes ½ inch thick. Place in a steamer rack set over a saucepan of rapidly simmering water, cover, and steam for 10 minutes, or until tender. Transfer to a medium bowl and mash until smooth, then set aside.

In a small saucepan over medium high heat, combine the sugar with 1 cup of water and bring to a boil. Continue to boil for 10 minutes, or until the mixture forms a golden brown syrup. Immediately remove the caramelized sugar from the heat and divide it among six timbale molds or ramekins (see Note). Swirl the ramekins to distribute the caramelized sugar evenly around the bottoms and lower sides. Allow to cool.

In a large bowl, combine the eggs, cream, salt, a pinch of pepper, and a pinch of nutmeg. Add the mashed sweet potatoes and mix thoroughly.

Butter the sides of the ramekins and fill them with the sweet potato custard mixture. Place the ramekins in a baking dish and add enough hot water to reach halfway up the sides of the ramekins. Cover the baking dish with aluminum foil and bake the timbales for 30 minutes, or until the custard is firmly set.

To serve, invert each timbale onto a plate.

Note: Timbale molds are slightly taller and narrower than standard ramekins.

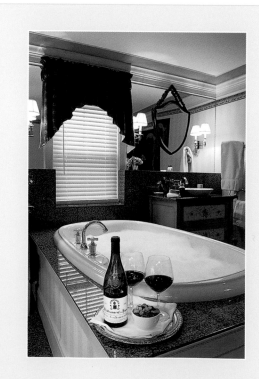

THE SPACIOUS WHIRLPOOL BATHS
IN THE WHITE BARN INN'S SUITES PROVIDE
THE PERFECT PLACE TO SOAK AWAY
THE STRESS OF EVERYDAY LIFE AND ENJOY AN
AFTERNOON OF PAMPERING.

Tenderloin of Beef Glazed in a Foie Gras Crust on a Potato Rösti with Madeira Sauce

*This wonderfully wintery beef entrée is a perfect alternative
to the venison recipe. The golden foie gras crust adds another level of richness
and flavor to an already superb cut of beef. Crisp potato rösti, a lovely contrast
in texture, provide a perfect foil for the Madeira sauce. Hearty vegetables
such as cauliflower or carrots tossed in oil and roasted until tender in a 400°F oven
make a nice accompaniment to this dish. Foie gras crust can be stored up
to 5 days in the refrigerator and makes a superb topping for mashed potatoes. If you
prefer, substitute the Pepper Crust on page 240 for the foie gras crust.*

Serves 4

4 ounces diced fresh foie gras or foie gras terrine (about $\frac{1}{2}$ cup)

$10\frac{1}{2}$ tablespoons unsalted butter, at room temperature

$\frac{2}{3}$ cup grated Vermont cheddar cheese

3 tablespoons grated Parmesan cheese

$\frac{1}{2}$ cup fresh bread crumbs

Salt and freshly ground black pepper to taste

$\frac{1}{4}$ cup diced mixed aromatic vegetables
(onion, carrot, and leek)

$\frac{1}{8}$ cup Madeira

$\frac{1}{4}$ cup port

2 crushed black peppercorns

2 cups Veal Jus (see page 68)

4 beef tenderloin filets (7 ounces each)

1 tablespoon olive oil

4 Potato Rösti (see page 231)

In a large bowl, combine the foie gras, 6 tablespoons of butter, the grated cheeses, and bread crumbs and mix until thoroughly combined. Season to taste with salt and pepper. Form the mixture into a ball and place it on a sheet of waxed paper. Roll the ball into a 3-inch cylinder and wrap it tightly in the waxed paper. Reserve in the refrigerator for up to 5 days, until ready to slice and use.

In a medium saucepan, melt 4 tablespoons of the remaining butter over medium heat. Add the mixed vegetables and sauté for 5 minutes, until the onion is translucent but not browned. Add the Madeira, port, and crushed peppercorns and cook at a low simmer over medium heat for 5 minutes, or until reduced by half. Add the Veal Jus and continue to cook at a low boil for 5 minutes, or until the sauce is reduced by half and coats the back of a spoon. Strain through a fine sieve and season to taste with salt and pepper.

Preheat the broiler. Season the beef filets with salt and pepper and roll them in the olive oil. Heat a large skillet over high heat. Add the beef and sear for 5 minutes on each side. Add the remaining $\frac{1}{2}$ tablespoon of butter to the pan and continue to cook over high heat for 3 to 5 minutes on each side for medium-rare beef. For medium beef, cook for 7 to 8 minutes on each side.

Divide the foie gras crust into four slices, place a slice on top of each filet, and place under the broiler for 1 to 2 minutes, just until the crust turns golden brown and begins to bubble.

To serve, place a Potato Rösti in the center of each plate. Top with a beef filet and spoon the sauce over the beef and potatoes.

Potato Rösti

These golden, butter-crisped potato pancakes
are easy to make and hard to resist.
If you are serving hearty eaters, you might double
this recipe and give each diner two rösti.

Makes 4

2 medium Yukon Gold potatoes, peeled and grated

Salt and freshly ground black pepper

1 tablespoon blended oil (see Note)

2 tablespoons unsalted butter

Squeeze any moisture out of the grated potatoes and season with salt and pepper. Using a 3-inch circular mold, form four ½-inch-thick potato cakes, pressing to firm the cakes. Heat the oil in a large, nonstick sauté pan over medium high heat. When the oil reaches the smoking point, slide the potato cakes into the pan. Reduce the heat to medium and add the butter. Cook the rösti for 3 to 4 minutes on each side, until golden brown. Remove from the pan and drain on paper towels before serving.

Note: Blended oil is a mixture of 90 percent vegetable oil and 10 percent olive oil.

WARM CHOCOLATE CAKE WITH WARM CHOCOLATE SAUCE AND VANILLA BEAN ICE CREAM

Who can resist a warm chocolate cake with a molten center—especially when paired with homemade Vanilla Bean Ice Cream? Since all the components of this dessert can be made several days in advance, it's a perfect way to end a festive winter meal. Just put the cakes into the oven when you serve the main course, and they will be ready to devour when it's time for dessert.

Serves 8

Warm Chocolate Sauce (see page 234)

Butter and sugar for preparing the ramekins

10 ounces semisweet chocolate

$5/8$ pounds ($2\frac{1}{2}$ sticks) unsalted butter

5 large eggs

5 egg yolks

$\frac{1}{3}$ cup sugar

$\frac{3}{4}$ cup sifted all-purpose flour

Vanilla Bean Ice Cream (see page 235)

Prepare the Warm Chocolate Sauce and set aside.

Butter eight shallow 4-ounce ramekins, sprinkle with sugar, and set aside.

Combine the chocolate and butter in the top of a double boiler over low heat or in a microwave at half power until the chocolate melts. Allow to cool slightly.

In a large bowl, combine the eggs, egg yolks, and sugar. Using an electric mixer, beat for about 5 minutes, until the mixture is very pale yellow in color and falls in flat ribbons when the beaters are lifted. Fold in the chocolate mixture, then fold in the flour.

Divide the batter evenly among the eight molds and reserve until ready to bake. Unbaked cakes will keep at room temperature for up to 1 hour and in the refrigerator for up to 5 hours.

Thirty minutes before serving, preheat the oven to 375°F.

Bake the cakes for 10 minutes if at room temperature (20 minutes if they have been refrigerated). Allow the cakes to rest for about 5 minutes after removing from the oven, then invert them onto warmed dessert plates. Serve with Warm Chocolate Sauce and Vanilla Bean Ice Cream.

WARM CHOCOLATE SAUCE

Drizzling this rich, dark sauce over
chocolate cake is gilding the lily, but that is what
holiday dinner parties are all about.
You can also serve this with ice cream alone or over
Poached Pears (see page 256) and ice cream.

Makes 2 cups

1 cup milk

1 cup sugar

1⅓ cups Dutch cocoa

4 ounces good-quality semisweet chocolate

In a large, heavy-bottomed saucepan, combine the milk, sugar, cocoa, and chocolate with 1 cup of water over medium low heat, whisking frequently. When the chocolate melts and the mixture comes to a boil, remove it from the heat. Serve warm or reserve and reheat gently before serving. The sauce will keep for 1 hour at room temperature or for 2 to 3 days, covered and refrigerated.

Vanilla Bean Ice Cream

It's hard to beat the flavor of a homemade ice cream prepared with heavy cream and plenty of fresh vanilla bean— especially when paired with Warm Chocolate Sauce.

Makes 1½ quarts

2 cups milk

2 cups heavy cream

1 cup sugar

1 vanilla bean, split lengthwise

8 egg yolks

In a large saucepan with a heavy bottom, combine the milk, cream, ½ cup of sugar, and the vanilla bean, scraping out the seeds with a teaspoon and adding them as well as the bean halves to the pan. Bring to a simmer over medium heat.

In a large heat-resistant bowl, combine the remaining ½ cup of sugar with the egg yolks and stir to combine.

Pour ½ cup of the hot milk and cream into the sugar-and-egg-yolk mixture and stir to mix. Whisking constantly, slowly add the remainder of the hot milk and cream (including the vanilla bean) to the bowl.

Return the mixture to the pan and cook over medium heat, stirring constantly, until the mixture thickens enough to coat the back of a wooden spoon. If you can run your finger down the back of the spoon and leave a trail, the custard is done. Do not allow the mixture to boil.

Strain the custard through a fine sieve into a clean bowl and refrigerate until chilled. Freeze in an ice cream machine, following the manufacturer's instructions.

A Holiday Cocktail Party

The White Barn Inn hosts a cocktail party for its Christmas Prelude guests, many of whom come year after year to launch their holiday season with a festive weekend in Kennebunkport. Champagne corks pop and silver trays full of canapés are passed while old friends and new gather to celebrate. This menu brings together several favorite recipes that highlight the winter flavors of Maine's shellfish and game.

NORTHERN LIGHTS COCKTAIL

Linda Allen, bartender at the White Barn Inn, created
this champagne cocktail after witnessing the glow of northern lights
during a nighttime stroll on Gooch's Beach. A variation
on a kir royale, this mixture of pear purée, crème de cassis,
and champagne fills the champagne flute
with rosy translucence.

Makes 1 cocktail

1 ounce pear nectar

1 teaspoon crème de cassis

½ cup chilled champagne

Combine the ingredients in a cocktail shaker filled with ice. Stir until the shaker begins to turn frosty on the outside. Strain the mixture into a cocktail glass and serve immediately.

Maine Oyster Canapés

*Though labor intensive, oysters are well worth
the trouble of cleaning and shucking. To serve this dish at a cocktail party,
open the oysters just before guests arrive and keep them chilled on trays of ice;
garnishing takes only a few minutes. The Pepper Crust used as a topping
can be made several days in advance, so the baked oysters can also be prepared and
glazed in a matter of minutes. If you prefer to keep things simpler,
just prepare one or two variations. For this recipe I use local Glidden Point oysters,
which are cultivated above the ocean bed, so they are not gritty at all.
However, any good-quality medium to large oyster
with plump, flavorful flesh will work well.*

Makes 20 canapés

½ cup crème fraîche or sour cream

1 tablespoon prepared horseradish

Salt and freshly ground pepper

1 teaspoon wasabi powder

20 medium or large oysters, cleaned and shucked,
with bottom shells reserved

4 small sprigs fresh dill

4 small sprigs fresh chervil

8 slices Pepper Crust (see page 240)

1 tablespoon golden osetra
or regular osetra caviar (see Note)

Coarse kosher salt (optional)

In a small bowl, combine ¼ cup of crème fraîche with the horseradish and season
to taste with salt and pepper.

In another small bowl, mix the wasabi powder with a few drops of water to form
a smooth paste. Combine with the remaining 4 tablespoons of crème fraîche.

Preheat the oven to 450°F.

Remove four oysters from their bottom shells and place a tablespoon of the wasabi-crème fraîche mixture into the shell. Replace the oysters on top and garnish with dill sprigs.

Remove four more oysters from their bottom shells and place a tablespoon of the horseradish-crème fraîche mixture into the shell. Replace the oysters on top and garnish with chervil sprigs.

Top four more oysters with $\frac{1}{2}$ teaspoon of crème fraîche and $\frac{1}{4}$ tablespoon of the caviar.

Place the remaining eight oysters in a shallow baking dish. Cut eight $\frac{1}{4}$-inch slices of Pepper Crust and arrange on top of the oysters. Bake these oysters for 3 minutes, until the crust turns golden brown and starts to bubble.

While baking the oysters, divide the raw oysters among serving plates or arrange them on a large serving platter. A bed of lightly moistened course kosher salt can be used to keep the oysters level. Add the baked oysters to the serving plates or platter and serve at once.

Note: Golden osetra caviar is better in quality and lighter in color than regular osetra caviar; you can substitute any type of good-quality caviar.

Pepper Crust

This crust, made with Parmesan and butter and seasoned
with mild-flavored green and pink peppercorns, is rich and subtly piquant.
In addition to making a wonderful topping for baked oysters,
it also forms a delicious glaze for salmon and beef filets. Just cover a cooked filet
with a slice or two of the crust and run under a preheated broiler for one
to two minutes, until the crust is hot and bubbling.

Makes about 30 slices

¼ pound grated Parmesan cheese (about ¾ cup)

½ pound (2 sticks) unsalted butter, at room temperature

2 tablespoons green peppercorns, drained

4 tablespoons pink peppercorns

½ pound fresh bread crumbs (about 4 cups)

Salt and freshly ground black pepper

In a large bowl, combine all of the ingredients and mix until thoroughly blended. Season to taste with salt and pepper. Form the mixture into a ball and place it on a sheet of waxed paper. Roll the ball into a cylinder 2 inches in diameter and wrap it tightly in the waxed paper. Reserve in the refrigerator for up to 2 weeks.

PAN-SEARED NORTH ATLANTIC SHRIMP AND QUAIL EGG CANAPÉS

North Atlantic deep sea shrimp caught off the Massachusetts coast are crisp and sweet. If you can't find them, just use the freshest shrimp available. At the White Barn Inn's holiday party, we pass these on silver spoons. Garnished with a tiny quarter of hard-cooked quail egg, they make a perfect bite-size canapé. If you can't find quail eggs, a hard-cooked hen's egg, finely diced, may be substituted.

Make 8 canapés

2 quail eggs

1 tablespoon ketchup

1 teaspoon grated horseradish

Salt and freshly ground black pepper

1 teaspoon butter

8 small shrimp, peeled and deveined

8 small sprigs fresh dill

Bring a small saucepan of water to a boil over high heat. Add the quail eggs, reduce the heat to medium, and simmer for 2½ minutes. Cool to room temperature, peel, and cut into quarters with a sharp knife.

In a small bowl, combine the ketchup and horseradish and season to taste with salt and pepper.

Melt the butter in a small skillet over medium high heat. Add the shrimp and sear for 1 to 2 minutes, until firm and pink.

Divide the horseradish sauce among eight dessert spoons. Place a seared shrimp on each spoon. Top with the quartered quail eggs and garnish with dill sprigs.

DUCK CONFIT AND APPLE PASTIES

In England, hot pastry pockets stuffed with savory meat fillings
called pasties *are a winter favorite. These little pasties encase tender bits*
of duck confit sweetened with diced apples. They can be prepared
up to a month in advance and frozen, making them a perfect holiday food
to keep on hand for small cocktail gatherings or big parties.

Makes 8 pasties

1 tablespoon unsalted butter

1 McIntosh apple, peeled, cored, and diced

2 legs duck confit (see page 243),
about 8 ounces on the bone, skinned, boned, and diced

1 tablespoon apple cider

1 pound frozen puff pastry, thawed

1 egg, beaten

Preheat the oven to 350°F.

In a medium skillet, melt the butter over medium heat. Add the diced apple and sauté for 2 to 3 minutes, until the apple begins to soften. Add the duck confit and the apple cider and sauté for 2 minutes, until the apple is completely tender but still holds its shape. Remove from the heat and cool to room temperature.

On a cool, floured surface, roll out the puff pastry ⅛ inch thick. Using a 1½-inch fluted cutter, cut sixteen rounds of pastry. Place 1 teaspoon of the duck-and-apple mixture on eight of the rounds. Using a pastry brush, brush the beaten egg on the pastry around the filling. Top with the remaining eight rounds of pastry and press the outer edges together to form a firmly sealed packet. Refrigerate for up to three days before baking.

Place the pasties on a buttered baking sheet and bake for 10 to 12 minutes, or until puffed and golden brown. Serve hot.

Unbaked pasties may be frozen on a baking sheet and then stored in an airtight container in the freezer. Defrost for 30 minutes and bake for 13 to 16 minutes, until puffed and golden brown.

Duck Confit

Duck confit is available in some gourmet stores and through mail order, but it is also fairly easy to make and is a great way to use leftover legs when preparing a recipe that calls only for the duck breast. To render the duck fat called for in this recipe, trim the fatty parts of the duck and bring to a low boil, along with ½ cup of water, in a saucepan over a medium heat for about 20 minutes. Let cool slightly, strain, and refrigerate. Leftover duck fat will keep, tightly covered, in the refrigerator for two weeks and makes an excellent medium for searing poultry, as it has a very high smoke point. It is also useful as a protective layer for homemade pâtés and meat terrines.

Makes 2 legs

2 duck legs

½ cup kosher salt

1 sprig fresh thyme

2 black peppercorns

1 clove garlic

½ cup duck fat or olive oil

In a small nonreactive glass or stainless steel bowl, combine the legs with the salt, thyme, peppercorns, and garlic, rubbing the salt to coat the legs evenly. Cover and refrigerate for 24 hours.

After 24 hours, rinse the salt thoroughly off the legs, reserving the thyme, peppercorns, and garlic.

Preheat the oven to 250°F.

Place the legs, thyme, peppercorns, and garlic in a small casserole and cover with duck fat or olive oil or a mixture of both. Bring to a boil over medium high heat.

Remove the casserole from the heat, cover loosely with waxed paper or a lid, and bake for about 2 hours. To test for doneness, slide a roasting fork into the meat. If the meat drops easily off the fork, it is done.

If cooked in duck fat, the duck legs can be covered with the fat and packed in an airtight container for up to 2 weeks in the refrigerator; if cooked in olive oil, they will keep for up to 1 week. The legs can also be drained, boned, and frozen in an airtight container, reserving the duck fat for another use.

FETA CHEESE
AND SPINACH ROLLS

These bite-size canapés are a cross between
Greek spanakopita and Asian eggrolls. They can be prepared
up to three days in advance and kept, uncooked,
in an airtight container in the refrigerator, or frozen uncooked
for up to a month. Just bring them to room temperature
before frying as instructed below.

Makes 12 canapés

1 teaspoon unsalted butter

½ red bell pepper, cored, seeded,
and finely diced

1 cup baby spinach leaves, washed

2 tablespoons feta cheese, crumbled

Salt and freshly ground black pepper

Pinch freshly grated nutmeg

3 (4 x 4-inch) spring roll wrappers

1 egg, beaten

2 cups canola oil

In a skillet, melt the butter over medium heat. Add the diced pepper and cook for 2 to 3 minutes, until it begins to soften. Increase the heat to high and add the spinach, cooking for another minute, stirring occasionally, until the spinach wilts. Cool to room temperature and squeeze out any excess moisture.

Transfer the mixture to a medium mixing bowl. Add the feta cheese, and season to taste with salt, pepper, and nutmeg, being careful not to oversalt, since the feta cheese has a high salt content.

Quarter the spring roll wrappers, making two perpendicular cuts. Lay the quarters on a clean work surface. Place a teaspoon of the feta mixture inside one corner of each wrapper quarter. Brush the opposite corner with the beaten egg. Fold the sides of the wrapper in to cover the filling and roll tightly, making sure the top is well sealed with the beaten egg.

Heat the oil to 350°F over medium high heat in a deep frying pan or an electric deep-fryer. Fry the rolls at 350°F for 3 minutes or until golden brown. Drain on paper towels and serve warm. If you prefer baking to frying, you can brush the rolls with oil and bake in a 350°F oven for 6 to 8 minutes, until golden brown and warmed through.

GRACIOUS DINNERS AT THE WHITE BARN INN OFTEN BEGIN WITH
SAVORY LITTLE BITE-SIZED CANAPES TO WHET THE APPETITE AND ACCOMPANY A COCKTAIL,
INCLUDING CRISP FETA CHEESE AND SPINACH ROLLS, A CROSS BETWEEN
GREEK SPANAKOPITA AND ASIAN EGG ROLLS.

MAINE PEEKIE TOE CRAB CAKES

Peekie toe crab is another name for the sand crabs that are plentiful along Maine's beaches.
These plump-clawed crabs yield tender, sweet flesh that is perfectly suited for crab cakes.
You will have a hard time making enough of these moist morsels to go around.

Makes 4 main-course servings or 16 canapés

8 ounces Maine peekie toe crabmeat or other white crabmeat

1 small shallot, diced

1 tablespoon fresh homemade mayonnaise (see page 108),
or a good-quality commercial brand

1 tablespoon chopped chives

1 large egg yolk

1 cup fine white bread crumbs

1 dash Tabasco sauce

Salt and freshly ground pepper

2 tablespoons flour

1 large egg

2 tablespoons blended oil (see Note)

In a medium mixing bowl, combine the crab, shallot, mayonnaise, chives, and egg yolk. Add 2 tablespoons of the bread crumbs and mix well. Add the Tabasco and season with salt and pepper. Shape the mixture into eight or sixteen crab cakes, depending upon whether you will be serving them as a main course or canapé.

Place the flour in a shallow bowl and season to taste with salt and pepper. Beat the egg in a separate shallow bowl. Place the remaining bread crumbs in a third shallow bowl. Dip each cake carefully in the seasoned flour, then the beaten egg, and finally in the bread crumbs, making sure it is completely coated in bread crumbs and retains its shape.

In a medium skillet heat the oil until it shimmers. Add the crab cakes, working in two batches, and fry until golden brown, 3 to 4 minutes on each side. Drain on paper towels and serve warm.

Note: Blended oil is a mixture of 90 percent vegetable oil and 10 percent olive oil.

Marinated Salmon Tartare with Golden Osetra Caviar

Made with salt- and citrus-cured salmon, this delicious tartare
retains the deep orange color and moist meatiness of just-caught salmon.
By forming the chopped salmon into oval-shaped individual portions,
and presenting them on spoons, you can keep the focus on the
tartare's intense flavor and succulent texture instead of serving it
on the more traditional toast or cracker.

Makes 8 canapés

¼ pound Citrus-Cured Salmon (see page 248)

1 teaspoon chopped fresh dill

1 teaspoon sour cream

1 teaspoon golden osetra caviar

Finely dice the cured salmon; you should have about ¾ cup. In a medium bowl, combine it with the dill. Divide the mixture into eight even portions. Using two tea-spoons, shape each portion into a rounded oval. Place each oval on a clean teaspoon. Garnish with sour cream and caviar and serve.

Cured with a mixture of salt, citrus peel and juices, gin, and juniper berry, this salmon has a bright, refreshing flavor. It is also a lot easier to make than cold-smoked salmon, which requires steady vigilance over the smoker. In addition to chopping it finely for tartare, you can also cut this salmon into thin slices and form the slices into rosettes for serving. It will keep tightly covered in the refrigerator for up to one week.

Makes 2 pounds

2 pounds Maine salmon filet, bones removed, with skin on

1 tablespoon olive oil

4 tablespoons sea salt

4 tablespoons sugar

½ teaspoon coarsely crushed black peppercorns

2 juniper berries

2 oranges

2 lemons

1 ounce gin

Chopped fresh dill (optional)

Place the salmon skin-side down in a shallow, nonreactive glass or stainless steel dish large enough to hold the filet flat. Rub the filet with the olive oil.

In a medium bowl, combine the salt, sugar, pepper, and juniper berries. Cover the salmon filet with this mixture, heaping more curing mixture on the thicker parts of the filet.

Peel the oranges and lemons, cutting the peel into slices about ½ inch wide and 1½ to 2 inches long. Cover the salmon with the peels.

Juice one orange and both lemons into a medium bowl. Stir in the gin and pour over the salmon. Cover the dish tightly with plastic wrap and refrigerate for 18 hours.

After 18 hours, rinse the salmon quickly under cold water to remove the peel and salt mixture. Pat dry with paper towels. If serving whole, slice thinly on the diagonal, arrange slices in an overlapping pattern on a serving platter, and garnish with chopped fresh dill.

A New Year's Day Brunch

New Year's Day tends to dwell in the shadow of New Year's Eve, yet it is a wonderful time to gather with family and friends. Many of the recipes for this colorful, flavorful brunch may be prepared days in advance, and several dishes can be served either warm or at room temperature, making them ideal for a buffet. While the scrambled eggs and French toast should be eaten hot, they can be prepared at the last minute and put on the table just before guests are summoned to fill their plates.

COLD-SMOKED MAINE SALMON WITH CREAMY SCRAMBLED EGGS

Well-scrambled eggs with a touch of cream and butter are always delicious.
Paired with thinly sliced smoked salmon, this simple dish
becomes both elegant and irresistible. Try to use free-range eggs when
making this dish, as the flavor is superior.

Serves 6

12 large free-range eggs

½ cup heavy cream

1 tablespoon unsalted butter

Salt and freshly ground pepper

1 pound Cold-Smoked Salmon, thinly sliced,
at room temperature (see page 91)

In a large mixing bowl, combine the eggs and cream and whisk until thoroughly combined and frothy.

In a large nonstick pan, melt the butter over medium heat. Add the egg-and-cream mixture and stir with a wooden spoon. Season with salt and pepper. Continue gently stirring the eggs for 4 to 6 minutes, or just until they form soft curds.

To serve, arrange the salmon and eggs attractively on a warmed serving platter or divide among six individual plates.

APPLE FRENCH TOAST

This French toast has a surprise inside: a pocket full of warm diced apple sautéed with apple brandy. For best results, buy an unsliced loaf of firm-textured white bread from an artisanal bakery. This recipe makes enough to serve six people as part of a larger brunch menu. If you are serving this alone, make enough for two slices per person.

Makes 6 pieces

6 (1-inch) slices firm white bread

3½ tablespoons unsalted butter

1 ½ cups peeled, cored and diced Granny Smith apples
(about 2 apples)

⅓ cup plus 1 ½ tablespoons sugar

3 tablespoons Calvados brandy

$\frac{1}{3}$ cup pure maple syrup

$\frac{3}{4}$ teaspoon ground cinnamon

6 eggs

$\frac{3}{4}$ cup heavy cream

Using a sharp knife, make a pocket in each slice of bread by cutting from the bottom of each piece to about 2 inches from the top.

In a sauté pan melt $1\frac{1}{2}$ tablespoons of the butter over medium heat. Add the apples and $1\frac{1}{2}$ tablespoons of sugar and sauté for 2 to 3 minutes, until the apples begin to soften. Add $1\frac{1}{2}$ tablespoons of the Calvados, $1\frac{1}{2}$ tablespoons of the maple syrup, and the cinnamon, and sauté 2 to 3 minutes longer, until the apple is completely tender but still holds its shape.

Divide the apple mixture into two equal parts, reserving half for the sauce and using the remaining half to fill the bread slices. Loosely pack the apple mixture into each bread pocket, pressing the edges of the bread together to seal.

In a medium mixing bowl, whisk together the eggs, cream, and remaining $\frac{1}{3}$ cup of sugar.

Melt the remaining 2 tablespoons of butter in a large skillet over medium heat. Gently dip the bread slices in the batter and slide them into the skillet. Sauté, turning once, until golden brown, 3 to 5 minutes per side.

In a small saucepan, combine the reserved apple compote with the remaining Calvados and maple syrup and bring to a boil over medium heat. Remove from the heat. To serve, slice the pieces of French toast diagonally and arrange on a serving platter. Drizzle with sauce and serve additional sauce on the side.

Pineapple Coconut Granola

Granola is full of satisfying flavors and textures.
Served with fresh fruit, or poached fruits like those included in this menu,
it is a healthful addition to a brunch buffet. Don't be surprised
if your guests ask for this recipe.

Serves 10

4 cups unsweetened bran flakes

2 cups rolled oats

2 cups sliced unsalted almonds

1½ cups sweetened coconut

1 cup well-drained crushed pineapple

½ cup honey

Preheat the oven to 200°F.

In a very large bowl, combine all the ingredients and mix well with a wooden spoon until thoroughly combined. Transfer the mixture to two baking sheets and bake for 20 minutes.

After 20 minutes, stir the granola and open the oven door by about 6 inches to allow steam to escape and the granola to dry. Continue baking with the door ajar for 1 hour more, stirring every 20 minutes to ensure even baking. The granola is done when it is no longer damp but slightly chewy.

Remove the granola from the oven and cool on the baking sheets. It will continue to dry as it cools. Transfer to an airtight container, where it can be stored at room temperature for up to 10 days.

HAM AND
MOZZARELLA QUICHE

*Quiche is a great make-ahead dish that also works well on a buffet table,
as the flavor and texture hold up even at room temperature.
Feel free to add lightly cooked, well drained vegetables, such as spinach,
asparagus, onions, or mushrooms to this recipe. You can bake the crust up to
two days in advance and keep it covered in the refrigerator. The filling
is easily assembled while the oven preheats. While quiche tastes best hot out
of the oven, it can also be baked ahead and frozen. Bring it to
room temperature, then reheat it, loosely covered, in a microwave
oven for 90 seconds, or until heated through.*

Makes 1 (12-inch) quiche

2½ cups all-purpose flour

½ teaspoon salt

⅜ pound (1½ sticks) unsalted butter,
chilled and cut into pieces

10 eggs

4¼ cups heavy cream

2½ cups shredded mozzarella cheese

1½ cups diced ham

Salt and freshly ground pepper

In a large mixing bowl, combine the flour and salt. Using a pastry blender or two knives, cut the butter into the dry ingredients to form a fine cornmeal consistency. Gradually add ½ cup of cold water, mixing until a stiff dough forms. Let the dough rest in the refrigerator for 30 minutes.

Preheat the oven to 350°F.

Roll out the dough ¼ inch thick. Lifting it carefully, transfer to a 12-inch quiche pan with a removable bottom. Let the crust overlap the edges of the pan to prevent it from shrinking during baking. Bake for 30 minutes, using aluminum pie weights or dried beans to prevent the crust from rising and forming bubbles. The crust is done when the bottom is golden brown.

In a large bowl, beat the eggs until the yolks and whites are well combined. Add the cream and mix well. Season with salt and pepper. Evenly sprinkle the cheese and ham across the bottom of the baked crust. Pour the egg-and-cream mixture over the filling. Bake for 1 hour and 15 minutes, or until the filling is firmly set.

Note: If your quiche pan is smaller or shallower than 2 inches, reduce the amount of filling accordingly.

POACHED PEARS

*Pears are often poached in red wine. Here, a crisply fruity Sauvignon Blanc
accentuates the fruit's delicate flavor and allows the pears to retain
their creamy color. These make a lovely brunch dish, whether as a first course alongside hot or cold cereal, or as a dessert, served with Vanilla Bean Ice Cream and
drizzled with Warm Chocolate Sauce (see pages 235 and 234).*

Makes 6 cups

1 cup fruity white wine, such as Sauvignon Blanc

½ cup sugar

1 lemon, sliced and seeded

5 Bartlett pears

In a large saucepan, combine the wine, sugar, and lemon slices with 2 cups of water.
Peel, core, and quarter the pears, placing the pieces immediately into the saucepan
to prevent them from turning brown. Bring to a boil over high heat. Once the liquid comes to a boil, remove the pan from the heat and allow it to cool. Chill until
ready to serve. The pears can be made in advance and stored in a covered nonreactive glass or stainless container for up to three days.

AT THE RESTAURANT BAR, RUSTIC WOODEN BEAMS
ORIGINAL TO THE BARN CONTRAST WITH
SOFTLY GLEAMING METAL VENEER CREATED BY A
LOCAL METALSMITH, WHO WAS INSPIRED BY THE SLEEK
ELEGANCE OF ART MODERNE DESIGN.

PRUNES POACHED
WITH CINNAMON AND PORT

Dried plums, better known as prunes, are an overlooked fruit.
Poached in a mixture of red wine, port, and cinnamon, the prunes become plump,
moist, and delicious. Guests who might have passed up a serving of plain dried
or stewed prunes will come back for seconds of these. For an elegant dessert, top these
with Vanilla Bean Ice Cream (see page 235) and serve with a glass of cognac.

Makes 3 cups

1 pound pitted prunes (about 2½ cups)

1 cup red wine

½ cup port

1 (3-inch) stick cinnamon

1 orange, sliced and seeded

Combine all of the ingredients in a large saucepan and bring to a boil over
high heat. Remove the pan from the heat and allow the contents to cool.
Chill until ready to serve. The prunes may be refrigerated in a covered nonreactive glass or stainless steel container for up to three days.

Winter Ingredients

CABBAGE

Cabbage is a hearty vegetable that continues to thrive in cold weather; it even grows beneath a layer of winter's snow. Thinly sliced and lightly sautéed, it adds crunch and color to many dishes. The German tradition of marinating cabbage in wine lends even more flavor to this satisfying winter ingredient.

CELERIAC

Celeriac, also known as celery root, combines the delicate taste of celery stalks with the earthy flavor and texture of a root vegetable. Simmered or steamed until tender, it can be whipped into purées or incorporated into velvety-textured cream-based soups.

CHESTNUTS

Chestnut trees were plentiful in Maine before the onslaught of a blight that decimated the trees in the early twentieth century. Fortunately, some trees continue to grow in Maine, dropping nuts encased in a spiny outer shell in late autumn. The meat of the chestnut is moist and rich in flavor, delicious hot off the fire or puréed for a side dish or a full-bodied soup.

OYSTERS

Maine's cold waters harbor some of the most delicious oysters in the country, ranging in size from compact to plump, and in flavor from sweet to salty. Edible year-round, they have the best taste and texture in winter. Whether served raw, lightly poached, or baked in the shell, oysters are always a festive addition to the table.

POTATOES

Maine is home to more than 500 potato farms, many of which are located in northernmost Aroostook County. Maine farmers raise a wide variety of potatoes, including common russets, popular Yukon Golds, Russian banana fingerlings, and exotic blue varieties. Steamed, boiled, baked, fried, or sautéed, they never fail to satisfy winter cravings for hearty food.

SWEET POTATOES

These beautifully colored tubers are popular in cold and warm climates alike. Whether further sweetened with maple syrup or brown sugar, or served in savory presentations with herbs and a touch of garlic, sweet potatoes make a colorful and flavorful addition to winter meals.

VENISON

Thanks to the increasing availability of farm-raised venison, this lean and full-flavored meat can now be purchased fresh year-round. The perfect complement to winter's mellow root vegetables, venison is a cold-weather favorite on the menu of the White Barn Inn.

Source Guide

More and more supermarkets are carrying exotic produce, fresh shellfish, and other foods called for in some of the recipes in this book. Here are a few sources for mail-order and online shopping.

QZINA
83 Meyer Street
Hackensack, NJ 07601
Phone: 201–996–1939
www.Qzina.com

This online gourmet market favored by professional chefs carries crème pâtissière powder, griottes in syrup, kalamansi purée, fine chocolate, and many other products.

STONEWALL KITCHEN
Stonewall Lane
York, Maine 03909
Phone: 207–351–2713
www.stonewallkitchen.com

This specialty foods company makes jams, jellies, and marmalades, including Maine wild blueberry jam.

D'ARTAGNAN
280 Wilson Avenue
Newark, NJ 07105
Phone: 800–327–8246
www.dartagnan.com

Venison rib racks and tenderloins, whole guinea hens, guinea hen breasts, pheasant, foie gras, and other game meats and specialty foods, including truffle oil, truffles, forest mushrooms, and prepared chestnuts, are available from this top-quality purveyor, a favorite with restaurant chefs around the world.

EARTHY DELIGHTS
1161 East Clark Road, Suite 260
DeWitt, Michigan 48820 USA
Phone: 800–367–4709
www.earthy.com

Caviar and foie gras, Austrian pumpkin seed oil, truffles, fresh wild mushrooms, and artisanal goat cheeses are among the products available from this specialty foods company.

SPARROW ENTERPRISES
Phone: 800–783–4116
www.chocolatebysparrow.com

This gourmet chocolate company offers online access to the finest quality chocolate and fruit purées.

HARBOR FISH MARKET, INC.
9 Custom House Wharf
Portland, Maine 04101
Phone: 800–370–1790
Within Maine: 207–775–0251
www.cascobaybiz.com/harborfishmarket

This retail and online mail-order source offers the highest-quality native diver-harvested scallops, live lobsters, oysters, mussels, clams, farm-raised and wild salmon, and other seafood products (note: some items are only available in season).

THE LOBSTER COMPANY
1272 Portland Road, Route 1
Arundel, ME 04046
Phone: 207–985–3456

This seafood store offers fine Maine seafood, including live lobster, diver-harvested scallops, oysters, mussels, clams, and fish. Shipping not available.

SIMPLY SEAFOOD SUPERSTORE
1111 NW 45th St. Suite B
Seattle, WA 98107
877–706–4022

This Seattle-based company offers a retail location and an internet catalog for mail-ordering George's Bank giant sea scallops, Maine lobster, Pacific oysters, Pacific salmon, and other fresh seafood products.

THE GREAT CHEESES OF NEW ENGLAND
www.newenglandcheese.com

This web site, sponsored by The Great Cheeses of New England, New England Dairy Promotion Board, includes comprehensive information about New England cheese and cheese makers, including extensive details about how to purchase cheese online and in retail stores across the country.

WILLIAMS-SONOMA
Phone: 877–812–6235
www.williams-sonoma.com

With retail stores in major cities around the country and an online catalog with mail order service, this company offers ready access to cookware, bakeware (including timbale molds and ramekins), gourmet oils and vinegars, meat glazes, and more.

PREVIN INC.
2044 Rittenhouse Square
Philadelphia, PA 19103
Phone: 215–985–1996
www.previninc.com

Upon request, this company, specializing in supplying fine restaurants with kitchen and baking equipment, will ship individual items by mail, including bûche de noël molds, large quiche pans, timbale molds, and ramekins.

INDEX

A

Amuse Bouche
Carpaccio of Aged Tenderloin with a Szechuan Pepper and Soy Vinaigrette on a Salad of Beets and Daikon Radish, 23–25
Halibut, Hollandaise-Glazed Local, on Spring Fiddleheads and Forest Mushrooms, 27–29
Lobster on Mango Salsa with Golden Osetra Caviar and Lobster Mayonnaise, 217–218
Lobster Spring Roll with Carrot, Daikon Radish, and Snow Peas in a Thai-Inspired Spicy Sweet Sauce, 59–61
Pithiviers, Local Forest Mushroom and New England Goat Cheese, with Arugula and Herb Salad with Chanterelle Vinaigrette, 172–175
Scallops, Diver-Harvested, on Asparagus with Champagne Foam and Caviar, 57–58

Apple
and Duck Confit Pasties, 242
French Toast, 251–252

Apple Cider, Mulled, 197

Apricot Sorbet, 136

Arugula and Herb Salad with Chanterelle Vinaigrette, 174–175

Asparagus
Greens with Carrot Vinaigrette, Local Summer, 97–98
Salmon, Grilled, with Spring Fiddleheads, Scallions and, 50, 52
Scallops, Diver-Harvested, on, with Champagne Foam and Caviar, 57–58

Autumn
ingredients, 199
menus, 145–146
recipes, 147–198

Avocado and Lime Salsa, Tandoori-Crusted Soft Shell Crab with, 122–123

B

Baked Alaska, Black Cherry and Kirsch, 163–165

Barbecue Mayonnaise, 96

Bass, Pan-Roasted Striped, and Lobster Ravioli with Summer Zucchini Ribbons and Saffron Foam, 131–134

Beef
Tenderloin, Carpaccio of Aged, with a Szechuan Pepper and Soy Vinaigrette on a Salad of Beets and Daikon Radish, 23–25
Tenderloin of, Glazed in a Foie Gras Crust on a Potato Rosti with Madeira Sauce, 229–231

Beet
and Daikon Radish, Salad of, 25
Roasted, Ravioli of Butternut Squash, Pesto Potato and, on Spinach with Truffle Sauce, 178–182

Belgium Endive and Frisée Salad with Maine Goat Cheese and Grainy Mustard Vinaigrette, 170

Bell Pepper(s)
in Ratatouille, 34
Red, Roasted, Purée, 177
Red, Sorbet, 176

Berry(ies)
Muffins, Miniature, 112
See also names of berries

Beverages
Apple Cider, Mulled, 197
Glühwein, 212
Irish Coffee, 198
Lemonade, Homemade, 115
Rhubarb Smoothies, 49
See also Cocktails; Tea

Biscuits
Sablé, 187
Shortcake, 104

Bisque, Lobster, 77

Blueberry
Petits Fours, Warm, 121
Sorbet, 136

Breadsticks, Grissini, 209

Brussels Sprouts with Sautéed Shallots, 161

Buttermilk Ice Cream, 72

Butternut Squash
Cookies, 171
Ravioli of, Roasted Beet, Pesto Potato and, on Spinach with Truffle Sauce, 178–182

C

Cabbage, Red, Venison Cutlet, Pan Seared New England, with a Caramelized Sweet Potato Timbale, Elderberry Sauce and, 224–228

Cake
Chocolate Sponge, 165
Chocolate, Warm, with Warm Chocolate Sauce and Vanilla Bean Ice Cream, 233–235
Strawberry Shortcake, 103–105

Calamari, and Crispy Shrimp, Grilled Tournedos of Local Cod Loin with, on a Spring Pea Purée with a Piquant Sauce, 65–67

Canapés
Crab Cakes, Maine Peekie Toe, 246
Feta Cheese and Spinach Rolls, 244–245
Oyster, Maine, 238–239
Pasties, Duck Confit and Apple, 242
Salmon Tartare, Marinated, with Golden Osetra Caviar, 247
Shrimp, Pan-Seared North Atlantic, and Quail Egg, 241

Cantaloupe and Lychee Soup, Iced, 30

Carrot
Hummus Roll-Ups, 109–110
Lobster, Steamed Maine, Nestled on a Bed of Fettuccine with Ginger, Snow Peas, a Cognac Coral Butter Sauce and, 183–184
Lobster Spring Roll with Daikon Radish, Snow Peas and, in a Thai-Inspired Spicy Sweet Sauce, 59–62
Vinaigrette, 98

Caviar
Golden Osetra, Lobster on Mango Salsa with Lobster Mayonnaise and, 217–218
Golden Osetra, Marinated Salmon, Tartare with, 247
Scallops, Diver-Harvested, on Asparagus with Champagne Foam and, 57–58

Celeriac Soup, Truffled, 220–221

Champagne
Cocktail, Northern Lights, 236
Foam, Scallops, Diver-Harvested, on Asparagus with Caviar and, 57–58
Saffron Sauce, Salmon, Ragout of Maine, with Local Shellfish Medley and, 192–193
Strawberry, and Mandarin Orange Soup, 129
Strawberry Sorbet, 137
Truffle Cream Sauce, 181

Chanterelle Vinaigrette, Arugula and Herb Salad with, 174–175

Cheddar and Tomato Sandwiches, 116

Cheese
Cheddar and Tomato Sandwiches, 116
Feta Cheese and Spinach Rolls, 244–245
Goat Cheese, New England, and Forest Mushroom Pithiviers with Arugula and Herb Salad with Chanterelle Vinaigrette, 172–175
Mozzarella and Ham Quiche, 254–255
Red Currant Chutney with, 55
selection of artisanal, 53

Cherry(ies)
Bing, and Watermelon Soup, Iced, 92
Black, and Kirsch Baked Alaska, 163–165
Griotte Sorbet, 135

Chestnut(s)
    and Pheasant Soup, Velvety, 213–214
    Roasted, 210

Chicken Stock, 222

Chocolate
    Cake, Warm, with Warm Chocolate Sauce
        and Vanilla Bean Ice Cream, 233–235
    Sauce, Warm, 234
    S'Mores, 194–196
    Sponge, 165

Chocolate Chip Muffins, 80

Chutney, Red Currant, 55

Cilantro Oil, 62

Cinnamon
    Graham Crackers, 195
    Prunes Poached with Port and, 257

Clams
    in Shellfish, Medley, Local, and Saffron
        Champagne Sauce, Ragout of Maine
        Salmon with, 192–93
    in Shellfish and Corn Hash, Summer,
        126–127

Cocktails
    Cosmopolitan, Watermelon, 138
    Martinis, Edible, 89
    Northern Lights, 236
    Stars and Stripes, 56

Coconut Pineapple Granola, 253

Cod Loin, Grilled Tournedos of Local,
    with Crispy Shrimp and Calamari
    on a Spring Pea Purée with a
    Piquant Sauce, 65–67

Coffee, Irish, 198

Cognac Coral Butter Sauce, Steamed Maine
    Lobster Nestled on a Bed of Homemade
    Fetuccine with Carrot, Ginger, Snow
    Peas and, 183–184

Cookies, Butternut Squash, 171

Corn
    Salad, Grilled, 100
    and Shellfish Hash, Summer, 126–127

Cornbread for Stuffing, 156

Cosmopolitan, Watermelon, 138

Coulis, Tomato, Smoked, 128

Crab
    Cakes, Maine Peekie Toe, 246
    Tandoori-Crusted Soft Shell, with Avocado
        and Lime Salsa, 122–123

Crackers, Cinnamon Graham, 195

Cranberry Relish, 159
    Turkey Sandwich with Stuffing and, 168

Cream
    Five-Spice, 150
    Truffle Sauce, 181
    Whipped, Vanilla-Flavored, 105

Crème Brûlée, Poire William, on a Sable
    Biscuit and Pear Sorbet with Spiced Port
    Wine Sauce, 185–189

Crêpe Soufflé, Rhubarb, "Twice-Baked", with
    Buttermilk Ice Cream, 69–72

Crust
    Foie Gras, Tenderloin of Beef Glazed in a,
        on a Potato Rosti with Madeira Sauce,
        229–231
    Pepper, 240

D

Daikon Radish
    and Beet, Salad of, 25
    Lobster Spring Roll with Carrot,
        Snow Peas and, in a Thai-Inspired Spicy
        Sweet Sauce, 59–62

Desserts
    Baked Alaska, Black Cherry and Kirsch,
        163–165
    Chocolate Cake, Warm, with Warm
        Chocolate Sauce and Vanilla Bean Ice
        Cream, 233–235
    Cookies, Butternut Squash, 171
    Crème Brûlée, Poire William, on a Sable
        Biscuit and Pear Sorbet with Spiced Port
        Wine Sauce, 185–189
    Strawberry Shortcake, 103–105
    See also Ice Cream; Sorbet; Soufflé

Dessert Sauce
    Chocolate, Warm, 234
    Lemon, 46
    Port Wine, Spiced, 189

Dill-Infused Vodka, 92

Duck Confit, 243
    and Apple Pasties, 242

E

Egg(s)
    Poached, on Lobster Hash, 75–76
    Quail, and Shrimp, Pan-Seared North
        Atlantic, Canapés, 241
    Quiche, Ham and Mozzarella, 254–255
    Salad Sandwiches, 117
    Scrambled, Creamy, Cold-Smoked
        Maine Salmon with, 249
    See also Soufflé

Eggplant, Ratatouille, 34

Elderberry Sauce, Venison Cutlet, Pan Seared
    New England, with a Caramelized Sweet
    Potato Timbale, Red Cabbage and,
    224–228

Endive, Belgium, and Frisée Salad with
    Maine Goat Cheese and Grainy Mustard
    Vinaigrette, 170

F

Feta Cheese and Spinach Rolls, 244–245

Fettuccine, Lobster, Steamed Maine,
    Nestled on a Bed of, with Carrot,
    Ginger, Snow Peas, and a Cognac
    Coral Butter Sauce, 183–184

Fiddleheads, Spring
    about, 29, 81
    and Forest Mushrooms,
        Hollandaise-Glazed Local Halibut on,
        27–29
    Salmon, Grilled, with Asparagus, Scallions
        and, 50, 52

Fish
    Bass, Pan-Roasted Striped, and Lobster
        Ravioli with Summer Zucchini Ribbons
        and Saffron Foam, 131–134
    Cod Loin, Grilled Tournedos of Local, with
        Crispy Shrimp and Calamari on a Spring
        Pea Purée with a Piquant Sauce, 65–67
    Halibut, Hollandaise-Glazed Local,
        on Spring Fiddleheads and Forest
        Mushrooms, 27–29
    Tuna Loin, Grilled Yellowfin, on Summer
        Corn and Shellfish Hash with Smoked
        Tomato Coulis, 124–128
    See also Salmon

Five-Spice Cream, 150

Foie Gras Crust, Tenderloin of Beef Glazed
    in a, on a Potato Rosti with
    Madeira Sauce, 229–231

French Toast, 251–252

Frisée and Belgium Endive Salad with
    Maine Goat Cheese and Grainy
    Mustard Vinaigrette, 170

Fruit
    Bowl, Breakfast, 73
    See also names of fruits

G

Ginger, Crispy Fried, 150

Glühwein, 212

Goat Cheese, New England, and Forest
    Mushroom Pithiviers with Arugula
    and Herb Salad with Chanterelle
    Vinaigrette, 172–175

Graham Crackers, Cinnamon, 195

Granola, Pineapple Coconut, 253

Gravy, Turkey, Roasted Maine, with Sage and
    Onion Stuffing and, 154

Greens. *See* Salads; names of greens

Griotte Sorbet, 135

Grissini Breadsticks, 209

Guinea Hen
    Grilled Breast of, on Creamed Spinach
        with Potatoes, Spring Peas, and a
        Woodland Mushroom Sauce, 39–42
    Jus, 42

H

Halibut, Hollandaise-Glazed Local, on Spring Fiddleheads and Forest Mushrooms, 27–29

Ham and Mozzarella Quiche, 254–255

Hash
  Corn and Shellfish, Summer, 126–127
  Lobster, Poached Eggs on, 75–76
  Sweet Potato, 157

Hollandaise-Glazed Local Halibut on Spring Fiddleheads and Forest Mushrooms, 27–29

Hors d'Oeuvres. *See* Canapés

Hummus Carrot Roll-Ups, 109–110

I

Ice Cream
  Baked Alaska, Black Cherry and Kirsch, 163–165
  Buttermilk, 72
  Rosewater, 47
  Vanilla Bean, 235

Irish Coffee, 198

J

Jam, Strawberry, 120

Jus
  Guinea Hen, 42
  Veal or Lamb, 68

K

Kalamansi Sour Lemon Sorbet, 63

L

Lamb
  Herb-Roasted Spring, with Tomato Chardonnay Sauce on Ratatouille and Pesto Potato Purée, 31–38
  Jus, 68

Lemonade, Homemade, 115

Lemon Balm Soufflé and Rosewater Ice Cream, 43–47

Lemon Sauce, 46

Lime and Avocado Salsa, Tandoori-Crusted Soft Shell Crab with, 122–123

Lobster
  Bisque, 77
  Grilled Maine, with Barbecue Mayonnaise, Wild Rice Salad, and Grilled Corn Salad, 95–101
  Hash, Poached Eggs on, 75–76
  on Mango Salsa with Golden Osetra Caviar and Lobster Mayonnaise, 217–218
  Oil, 219
  Ravioli, 133–134

Roll, Maine, 106
Spring Roll with Carrot, Daikon Radish, and Snow Peas in a Thai-Inspired Spicy Sweet Sauce, 59–62
Steamed Maine, Nestled on a Bed of Homemade Fettuccine with Carrot, Ginger, Snow Peas, and a Cognac Coral Butter Sauce, 183–184
Stock, 78

Lychee and Cantaloupe Soup, Iced, 30

M

Madeira Sauce, Tenderloin of Beef Glazed in a Foie Gras Crust on a Potato Rosti with, 229–231

Mango Salsa, Lobster on, with Golden Osetra Caviar and Lobster Mayonnaise, 217–218

Marshmallows, 196

Martinis, Edible, 89

Mayonnaise
  Barbecue, 96
  Homemade, 108
  Lobster, Lobster on Mango Salsa with Golden Osetra Caviar and, 217–218

Melons
  Cantaloupe and Lychee Soup, Iced, 30
  Fruit Bowl, Breakfast, 73
  Watermelon and Bing Cherry Soup, Iced, 92
  Watermelon Cosmopolitan, 138

Meringue, Baked Alaska, Black Cherry and Kirsch, 163–164

Mozzarella and Ham Quiche, 254–255

Muffins
  Berry, Miniature, 112
  Blueberry Petits Fours, Warm, 121
  Chocolate Chip, 80
  Poppyseed, 79

Mushroom(s)
  Forest, and New England Goat Cheese Pithiviers with Arugula and Herb Salad with Chanterelle Vinaigrette, 172–175
  Forest and Spring Fiddleheads, Hollandaise-Glazed Local Halibut on, 27–29
  Salad, Warm Fall, with Sherry Vinaigrette, 190–191
  Sauce, Woodland, Grilled Breast of Guinea Hen on Creamed Spinach with Potatoes, Spring Peas and a, 39–42

Mussels
  in Corn and Shellfish Hash, Summer, 126–127
  in Shellfish, Medley, Local, Ragout of Maine Salmon with Saffron Champagne Sauce and, 192–93

N

Nuts
  Chestnuts, Roasted, 210
  Granola, Pineapple Coconut, 253
  Spiced, 207–208
  Spiced Pecans, 152

O

Oil
  Cilantro, 62
  Lobster, 219
  Parsley, 29

Onion and Sage Stuffing, 155–156

Orange(s)
  in Fruit Bowl, Breakfast, 73
  Mandarin, Strawberry, and Champagne Soup, 129

Oyster Canapés, Maine, 238–239

P

Parsley Oil, 29

Pasta. *See* Fettuccine; Ravioli

Pasties, Duck Confit and Apple, 242

Pea(s)
  Purée, Spring, Grilled Tournedos of Local Cod Loin with Crispy Shrimp and Calamari on a, with a Piquant Sauce, 65–67
  Spring, Grilled Breast of Guinea Hen on Creamed Spinach with Potatoes, a Woodland Mushroom Sauce and, 39–42

Peach Iced Tea, 111

Pear(s)
  Poached, 256
  Sorbet, 188

Pecans, Spiced, 152

Pepper
  Crust, 240
  Szechuan, and Soy Vinaigrette, 24

Pepper(s). *See* Bell Pepper(s)

Pesto, 36
  Potato, Ravioli of Butternut Squash, Roasted Beet and, on Spinach with Truffle Sauce, 178–182
  Potato Purée, 35

Pheasant
  and Chestnut Soup, Velvety, 213–214
  Roast, 214

Pineapple
  Coconut Granola, 253
  in Fruit, Bowl, Breakfast, 73

Piquant Sauce, 67

Pithiviers, Local Forest Mushroom and New England Goat Cheese, with Arugula and Herb Salad with Chanterelle Vinaigrette, 172–175

Poppyseed Muffins, 79

Port
  Prunes Poached with Cinnamon and, 257
  Wine Sauce, Spiced, 189

Potato(es)
  Chips, Herb, 38
  Guinea Hen, Grilled Breast of, on Creamed
    Spinach with Spring Peas, a Woodland
    Mushroom Sauce and, 39–42
  in Hash, Corn and Shellfish, Summer,
    126–127
  Pesto, Ravioli of Butternut Squash, Roasted
    Beet and, on Spinach with Truffle Sauce,
    178–182
  Pesto Purée, 35
  Rosti, 231
  Sticks, in Cod Loin, Grilled Tournedos of
    Local, with Crispy Shrimp and Calamari
    on a Spring Pea Purée with a Piquant
    Sauce, 65–67
  Whipped, 162

Prunes, Poached with Cinnamon and
  Port, 257

Pumpkin
  Seed Vinaigrette, An Autumn Assortment of
    Lettuces with Roquefort Cheese and
    Spiced Pecans in, 151–152
  Soup, with Seared Diver Scallops and
    Five-Spice Cream, 147–150
  Soup, Spiced, 167

Q

Quail Egg and Pan-Seared North Atlantic
  Shrimp Canapés, 241

Quiche, Ham and Mozzarella, 254–255

R

Radish. See Daikon Radish

Raspberry(ies)
  in Fruit Bowl, Breakfast, 73
  Iced Tea, 113–114

Ratatouille, 34

Ravioli
  of Butternut Squash, Roasted Beet,
    and Pesto Potato on Spinach with
    Truffle Sauce, 178–182
  Lobster, 133–134

Red Cabbage, Venison Cutlet, Pan Seared
  New England, with a Caramelized Sweet
  Potato Timbale, Elderberry Sauce and,
  224–228

Red Currant Chutney, 55

Red Pepper, Roasted
  Purée, 177
  Sorbet, 176

Relish
  Cranberry, 159
  Cranberry, Turkey Sandwich with Stuffing
    and, 168

Rhubarb
  Crêpe Soufflé, "Twice-Baked", with
    Buttermilk Ice Cream, 69–72
  Purée, 49
  Smoothies, 49

Rosewater Ice Cream, 47

S

Sablé Biscuits, 187

Saffron
  Champagne Sauce, Ragout of Maine
    Salmon with Local Shellfish Medley
    and, 192–193
  Foam, Pan-Roasted Striped Bass and
    Lobster Ravioli with Summer Zucchini
    Ribbons and, 131–134

Sage and Onion Stuffing, 155–156

Salads
  Arugula and Herb, with Chanterelle
    Vinaigrette, 174–175
  Beet and Daikon Radish, 25
  Belgium Endive and Frisée, with
    Maine Goat Cheese and Grainy Mustard
    Vinaigrette, 170
  Corn, Grilled, 100
  Fruit Bowl, Breakfast, 73
  Greens, with Carrot Vinaigrette, Local
    Summer, 97–98
  Lettuces in a Pumpkin Seed Vinaigrette
    with Roquefort Cheese and Spiced
    Pecans, An Autumn Assortment of,
    151–152
  Mushroom, Warm Fall, with Sherry
    Vinaigrette, 190–191
  Wild Rice, 101

Salmon
  Citrus-Cured, 248
  Cold-Smoked, 91
  Cold-Smoked, in Edible Martini, 89
  Cold-Smoked Maine, with Creamy
    Scrambled Eggs, 249
  Cold-Smoked, Sandwiches, 116
  Grilled, with Fiddleheads, Spring,
    Asparagus, and Scallions, 50, 52
  Ragout of Maine, with Local Shellfish
    Medley and Saffron Champagne Sauce,
    192–193
  Tartare, Marinated, with Golden Osetra
    Caviar, 247

Salsa
  Avocado and Lime, Tandoori-Crusted
    Soft Shell Crab with, 122–123
  Mango, Lobster on, with Golden Osetra
    Caviar and Lobster Mayonnaise,
    217–218

Sandwiches
  Carrot Hummus Roll-Ups, 109–110
  Egg Salad, 117
  Lobster Roll, Maine, 106

Salmon, Cold-Smoked, 116
S'Mores, 194–196
Tomato and Cheddar, 116
Turkey, with Stuffing and Cranberry
  Relish, 168

Sauces
  Champagne Foam, Scallops,
    Diver-Harvested, on Asparagus with
    Caviar and, 57–58
  Cognac Coral Butter, Lobster, Steamed
    Maine, Nestled on a Bed of Homemade
    Fettuccine with Carrot, Ginger, Snow
    Peas and, 183–184
  Elderberry, Venison Cutlet, Pan Seared
    New England, with a Caramelized
    Sweet Potato Timbale, Red Cabbage and,
    224–228
  Hollandaise-Glazed Halibut, Local,
    on Spring Fiddleheads and Forest
    Mushrooms, 27–30
  Madeira, Tenderloin of Beef Glazed in a
    Foie Gras Crust on a Potato Rosti with,
    229–231
  Mushroom, Woodland, Guinea Hen,
    Grilled Breast of, on Creamed Spinach
    with Potatoes, Spring Peas and a, 39–42
  Pesto, 36
  Piquant, 67
  Saffron Champagne, Salmon, Ragout of
    Maine, with Local Shellfish Medley and,
    192–193
  Saffron Foam, Striped Bass, Pan-Roasted,
    and Lobster Ravioli with Summer
    Zucchini Ribbons and, 131–134
  Thai-Inspired Spicy Sweet, 62
  Tomato Chardonnay, 37
  Truffle Cream, 181
  See also Dessert Sauce; Jus

Scallops
  on Asparagus with Champagne Foam
    and Caviar, Diver-Harvested, 57–58
  Seared Diver, and Five-Spice Cream,
    Pumpkin Soup with, 147–150
  in Shellfish and Corn Hash, Summer,
    126–127
  in Shellfish Medley and Saffron Champagne
    Sauce, Ragout of Maine Salmon with,
    192–193

Scones with Strawberry Jam, 119–120

Shellfish
  and Corn Hash, Summer, 126–127
  Medley, Local, and Saffron Champagne
    Sauce, Ragout of Maine Salmon with,
    192–93
  See also names of shellfish

Shortcake
  Biscuits, 104
  Strawberry, 103–105

Shrimp
  Crispy, and Calamari, Grilled Tournedos of
    Local Cod Loin with, on a Spring Pea
    Purée with a Piquant Sauce, 65–67
  Pan-Seared North Atlantic, and Quail Egg
    Canapés, 241

Smoked Salmon. *See* Salmon, Cold-Smoked

Smoothies, Rhubarb, 49

S'Mores, 194–196

Snow Peas
Lobster, Steamed Maine, Nestled on a Bed
of Fettuccine with Carrot, Ginger, a
Cognac Coral Butter Sauce and, 183–184
Lobster Spring Roll with Carrot, Daikon
Radish and, in a Thai-Inspired Spicy
Sweet Sauce, 59–62

Sorbet
Apricot, 136
Blueberry, 136
Griotte, 135
Kalamansi Sour Lemon, 63
Pear, 188
Red Pepper, Roasted, 176
Strawberry Champagne, 137

Soufflé
Lemon Balm, and Rosewater Ice Cream,
43–47
Rhubarb Crêpe, "Twice-Baked", with
Buttermilk Ice Cream, 69–72

Soups
Cantaloupe and Lychee, Iced, 30
Celeriac, Truffled, 220–221
Lobster Bisque, 77
Pheasant and Chestnut, Velvety, 213–214
Pumpkin, with Seared Diver Scallops and
Five-Spice Cream, 147–150
Pumpkin, Spiced, 167
Strawberry, Mandarin Orange, and
Champagne, 129
Watermelon and Bing Cherry, Iced, 92
See also Stock

Soy
Spicy Sweet Sauce, Thai-Inspired, 62
and Szechuan Pepper Vinaigrette, 24

Spinach
Creamed, Grilled Breast of Guinea Hen
on, with Potatoes, Spring Peas, and a
Woodland Mushroom Sauce, 39–42
and Feta Cheese Rolls, 244–245
Ravioli of Butternut Squash, Roasted Beet
and Pesto Potato on, with Truffle Sauce,
178–182

Spring
ingredients, 81
menus, 17–22
recipes, 23–79

Spring Roll(s)
Feta Cheese and Spinach, 244–245
Lobster, with Carrot, Daikon Radish, and
Snow Peas in a Thai-Inspired Spicy
Sweet Sauce, 59–62

Squash. *See* Butternut Squash; Yellow Squash

Stars and Stripes Cocktail, 56

Stock
Chicken, 222
Lobster, 78
Turkey, 160
Vegetable, 223

Strawberry(ies)
Jam, 120
Mandarin Orange, and Champagne Soup,
129
Marinated, 105
Shortcake, 103–105
Sorbet, Champagne, 137

Stuffing
Cornbread for, 156
Sage and Onion, 155–155
Turkey Sandwich with Cranberry Relish
and, 168

Summer
ingredients, 139
menus, 87–88
recipes, 89–138

Sweet Potato
Hash, 157
Timbale, Caramelized, 227–228

Szechuan Pepper and Soy Vinaigrette, 24

T

Tandoori-Crusted Soft Shell Crab with
Avocado and Lime Salsa, 122–123

Tea
Hunters', Christmas Present, 211
Iced, Peach, 111
Iced, Raspberry, 113–114

Thai-Inspired Spicy Sweet Sauce, 62

Tomato(es)
and Cheddar Sandwiches, 116
Coulis, Smoked, 128
Mayonnaise, Barbecue, 96
Sauce, Chardonnay, 37

Truffle(d)
Celeriac Soup, 220–221
Cream Sauce, 181

Tuna Loin, Grilled Yellowfin, on Summer
Corn and Shellfish Hash with Smoked
Tomato Coulis, 124–128

Turkey
Roasted Maine, with Sage and Onion
Stuffing and Gravy, 153–156
Sandwich with Stuffing and Cranberry
Relish, 168
Stock, 160
Sweet Potato Hash, 157

V

Vanilla
Ice Cream, Vanilla Bean, 235
Whipped Cream, -Flavored, 105

Veal, Jus, 68

Vegetable(s)
Ratatouille, 34
Stock, 223
See also names of vegetables

Venison Cutlet, Pan Seared New England,
with a Caramelized Sweet Potato
Timbale, Red Cabbage, and Elderberry
Sauce, 224–228

Vinaigrette
Carrot, 98
Chanterelle, Arugula and Herb Salad with,
174–175
Mustard, Grainy, Belgium Endive and
Frisée Salad with Maine Goat Cheese
and, 170
Pumpkin Seed, An Autumn Assortment of
Lettuces with Roquefort Cheese and
Spiced Pecans in, 151–152
Sherry, Mushroom Salad, Warm Fall, with,
190–191
Szechuan Pepper and Soy, 24

Vodka
Dill-Infused, 92
Martinis, Edible, 89
Stars and Stripes Cocktail, 56

W

Watermelon
and Bing Cherry Soup, Iced, 92
Cosmopolitan, 138

Whipped Cream, Vanilla-Flavored, 105

White Barn Inn
decor of, 7–8
history of, 6–7
Kennebunkport setting of, 8–10, 11, 13
local ingredients, 10–11
seasonal ingredients, 13–15

Wild Rice Salad, 101

Winter
ingredients, 258
menus, 205–206
recipes, 207–257

Y

Yellow Squash
in Ratatouille, 34
and Zucchini Ribbons, Summer,
Pan- Roasted Striped Bass and Lobster
Ravioli with Saffron Foam and, 131–134

Z

Zucchini
in Ratatouille, 34
Ribbons, Summer, Pan-Roasted Striped
Bass and Lobster Ravioli with Saffron
Foam and, 131–134